FINDING
Her

⟵ ⟶)•(⟶ ⟶

*A Journey Through the Monsters
That Tried to Break Me*

ANGIE LICKLITER

**LANDON
HAIL**
PRESS

Copyright© 2025 Angie Lickliter
All Rights Reserved

This book or any portion thereof may not be reproduced or used in any manner without the express written permission of the publisher, except for the use of brief quotations in a book review.

Paperback ISBN: 978-1-959955-62-7
Hardback ISBN: 978-1-959955-63-4

Cover design by Rich Johnson, Spectacle Photo
Book Cover Design by Angie Lickliter / Rich Johnson, Spectacle Photo
Photograph by Angelli Nguyen
Creative Direction by Samantha Joy

Published by Landon Hail Press

Although the author and publisher have made every effort to ensure the accuracy and completeness of information contained in this book, we assume no responsibility for errors, inaccuracies, omissions, or any inconsistency herein. Any slights on people, places, or organizations are unintentional. The material in this book is provided for educational purposes only. No responsibility for loss occasioned to any person or corporate body acting or refraining to act as a result of reading material in this book can be accepted by the author or publisher.

*This book is dedicated to my grandmother who resides in heaven. I can feel her presence as I write.
She once said....
"If you don't do it, you will never know.
If you do and fail, at least you'll know."
—Della Jane Anderson*

CONTENTS

Introduction 1
    The Warrior 1
    Enemies 3
    Battleground 4
SECTION 1: Her Monsters 5
Monster 1: Men 7
    Beneath the Surface 7
    The Groundbreaking News 10
    Boy, Oh Boy! 12
    Liking it Bad 19
    Bridezilla 23
    Braving the Storm Alone 30
    Stomping Grounds 33
    Split Decision 36
    Let's Get it On 38
    The Dirty Dating Pool and Number Two 42
    Third Time is a Charm 47
    Happily Ever After 49
Monster 2: Money 50
    Dollar Daze 50
    Off to Work I Go… Ho, Ho, Ho! 54
    Hidden Treasures 56

Dreams of Change	60
The Cash Crash	64
Dil-Dough	70
Coffee Currency	74
Barista Break	76
Back to the Grind	78
Holistic Dime Bags	80
Property Payoffs	84
From Pennies to Penmanship	86
Monster 3: Food	**92**
The Dreaded Dinner	92
Quick Fixes	94
Cafeteria Conundrum	95
The Diet Dilemma	98
Fork in the Road	106
Fatty Findings	109
Monster 4: The Mirror	**113**
Early Bloomer	113
The Distorted Reflection	115
Warrior Scars	118
Tan Lines	121
Covid Mid-Life Crisis	122
Monster 5: Alcohol	**126**
Brewing up Trouble	126
Adult Beverages	132
Liquid Courage	134
Boozy Beginnings	137
It's Wine O'clock Somewhere	141

Birthday Shots? No, Thanks! 146
   Sobering Truths 148
   Mocktail and Misconceptions..154
Monster 6: Gut 158
   Well, Crap! 158
   The Medical Merry Go Round..161
   Diverting without Doctors 167
   Name of the Beast..169
   Jumping Back on the Ride..172
   Now I Know my CBDs 176
   Excuse Me, WTF Did You Say? 180
   Bye-Bye Bowels 183
   Beyond the Battle...184
SECTION 2: Her Allies 189
Ally 1: Mom..191
Ally 2: Grandparents..195
Ally 3: Daughters...201
Ally 4: Husband 204
Ally 5: Tribe 207
Ally 6: Biological Father..210
SECTION 3: Her Weapons 217
Weapon 1: Books 219
   Money, Jobs and Business 220
   Food & Diet..220
   Mindset, Body Image and Self-Acceptance 221
   Alcohol..222
   Gut Health & Cannabis 221

- Weapon 2: Podcasts 223
  - Money, Jobs and Business...224
  - Food & Diet..224
  - Mindset, Body Image and Self-Acceptance 224
- Weapon 3: Meditation 225
  - YouTube 226
- Weapon 4: Yoga..227
  - YouTube 228
- Weapon 5: Workouts 229
  - Beachbody Programs 230
- Weapon 6: Mocktails...231
  - Beer..232
  - Liquor 232
  - Sparkling Wine 232
- Weapon 7: Cannabis 233
- SECTION 4: Her Sanctuaries 235
- Sanctuary 1: The Cabin...237
- Sanctuary 2: Herself 241
- SECTION 5: Final Reflections 245
- Acknowledgments 252
- About the Author 254

ANGIE LICKLITER

INTRODUCTION

THIS BOOK IS FOR ANYONE who's ever looked in the mirror and wondered where they went, for anyone who has buried pieces of themselves under years of responsibilities and survival, or who is simply trying to make it through the day. *Finding Her* isn't just about me. It's about all of us who have lost touch with the version of ourselves that once felt whole, powerful, and alive. This is not a guide filled with perfect answers. It's about digging deep, confronting the monsters I've tried to ignore, and finally saying: *enough*.

My hope is, in reading these pages, you'll feel seen, and you'll find the courage to face the parts of your story you are still struggling with and, in doing so, reclaim the life that has always been yours to live.

The Warrior

Finding Her wasn't always the title of this book. It began as *The Empty Pill Box*, a title that emerged during a meditation a few years ago. It was meant to capture my lengthy battle with Crohn's disease—my "Gut Monster," as I came to call it.

I watched my grandmother struggle with her health and her weight. I vividly recall her having a very full pill box. I vowed never to have one, myself. Hence, *The Empty Pill Box*. For a long time, I thought my greatest victory was healing my gut. And yes, that was a hard-earned triumph—years of misdiagnoses, medications, surgeries, and pain that stole too much from me. But as I peeled back the layers, I realized this important truth: my gut was only the beginning.

Looking back on the original title, I began to ponder the metaphor. Could it possibly be that the pills represented *all* of my monsters? And so, the empty, open box symbolized freedom from these monsters that were holding me back?

As the pen took over and the ink flowed, along with the tears, my real story was revealed.

The battle cries that came from sorrow and joy gave me the grit to go forth, while the box of tissue cleared my vision, so I could see the path. Before writing, I was immersed in a life of constant chaos. I truly didn't want to face the monsters, because, quite honestly, it was incredibly difficult.

What was truly mind-blowing is the self-discovery that developed on a journey I thought was simply about my gut. I considered professional counseling while I was writing this book, but then I realized the therapy was happening "write" in front of me. I quieted my mind, and, upon reflection, finding her became much easier

My story has not been a fairy tale, but I do consider myself fortunate for the life I have been given. I wake up grateful every day. This book isn't about placing blame or shaming anyone. The "bad things" that happen in our lives can teach us so much more than the good. These become our weapons. We gather them and build our arsenal to defend future "battles."

I am not a victim of my story. I am a warrior!

Enemies

Victories don't come without battles, and battles don't come without enemies. In *Finding Her*, those enemies weren't always what I'd expected. Some came dressed as self-doubt, comparison, guilt, or the need to please. Others lived inside old beliefs that told me I was too much or not enough. What guided me through them wasn't just willpower—it was instinct. Gut instinct. The same gut that had once felt broken and inflamed ended up being the very place where my truest self lived.

Let me introduce you to those enemies—The Monsters.

- **Men:** Comforted me at first, but while exiting, they took a portion of me that had fed my belief in needing someone else to fill the void.
- **Money:** Bankrolled me into believing I needed to prove my worth by what I earned.
- **Food:** Shoved me into a vicious cycle of comfort and struggle, as I searched for perfection that doesn't exist.
- **Mirror:** Showed me a reflection of whom I was *not*, but never whom I truly was, shattering my perception.
- **Alcohol:** Convinced me that a drink would make everything better, but, as the bottle emptied, so did I.
- **Gut:** Scared me the most, as it grew through the battles I had with the others.

Battleground

Each one of the chapters in this book starts off at the beginning of my life and leads you along a unique path, formed by each monster.

I do share my quirky, sometimes corny humor, which reveals itself in the names of each chapter's subsection. Battlegrounds can be tough, but if you can find the laughs in the process, it eases the burden and gives you the determination to keep going.

As the monsters persisted, so did my battle cries, which needed to be heard. These reflections are written in third person throughout my story. They are in present tense and set aside for you to find them clearly. In them, "she" is me as a person, and "her" my inner voice.

The quotes I share are some of my favorites, words that hit home as I forged on. Toward the end of the book, you will read about those that supported me, whom I call Allies. I will tell you some fun tales about them, along with explanations on how they helped me navigate the battlegrounds. The resource section, which I call Weapons, is next. These have been gathered along my war path, and I will direct you on how to obtain them, as well.

Finally, I will reveal how this part of my journey ended and where *she* found *her*. This is the best part, but no reading ahead!

Let this book be your guide, your inspiration, and your reminder that you are stronger than you think. So, if you're ready to confront your monsters and take back control of your life, let's begin this journey together. Victory is closer than you think.

SECTION 1

HER MONSTERS

"The staging for 'Monsters' is all about me getting free. In the beginning, I'm like tied in a dark place... until I am scared no more, and I'm taking the lead of my life, I'm being the queen of my life, I'm ruling the world! In the end, I'm taking a risk, but I'm taking the leap of faith."
—Saara Aalto

FINDING HER

Monster 1

Men

I HADN'T EVEN TAKEN my first breath before life handed me my first battle. That truth became a seed of rejection, and it grew wild in the soil of my soul.

Beneath the Surface

My journey began in Seattle, Washington, in April 1970. In a time when teenage pregnancy was far less accepted than it is today, my mother found herself pregnant and unmarried at just seventeen.

Her choices were the usual ones, each carrying its own consequence: keep the baby, give it up for adoption, or have an abortion. Her boyfriend at the time, my biological father, drove my mother to the abortion clinic and dropped her off.

The options available to women seeking abortions in Washington in the late 1960s were limited. Well-connected women could obtain legal, "therapeutic" abortions by convincing a hospital committee of physicians that the procedure was medically necessary. Wealthy women could travel to a foreign country where abortion was legal. One travel agency specialized in arranging trips to Japan, where, for $1,000, a woman could obtain a safe, legal abortion during a four-day stay that included one day for sightseeing. Less fortunate women could try to access an underground network of people willing to perform illegal abortions, and, if they were lucky, they *might* be referred to a skilled physician.

The clinic refused to perform the procedure on my mom. They told her she would have to go to Canada for an abortion. Unfortunately, this was not a viable option for my mom, because her parents didn't know, and there was no way to sneak away for that long without them finding out. She was left facing the reality that, in eight months, she would be a mother or she would have to gift her baby to another family.

In 1970, Referendum 20 legalized abortion for women "not quick with child" and within the "four lunar months after conception" Prior to Referendum 20, abortion was a criminal offense in Washington State, except in cases to preserve the mother's life. Once passed, this ballot measure required that, before an abortion could be performed, a married woman's husband must consent; when a woman was unmarried and under the age of eighteen, her parents had to give consent. Under Referendum 20, a woman also had to have resided in the state for at least ninety days before an abortion could be performed.

Thankfully, this referendum did not pass till the following year. Otherwise, I would not be alive! My mom sucked in her tummy and hid her baby bump until, in the seventh month of pregnancy, it became impossible to conceal. When I was seven months old, my mother married a man who legally adopted me. For now, I'll refer to him as my dad.

As you probably can imagine, my Men Monsters were more like daddy issues. While I do not want to use that cliché, I will share the meaning behind it here, in case you're not familiar, because this term explains a lot. As explained by Bisma Anwar, LMHC, in her *Ask a Therapist* article, "Do I Have Daddy Issues?" on Talkspace, "Daddy issues" is a phrase, often used disparagingly and refers to women who have complex, confusing, or dysfunctional relationships with men.

"It can describe people who project subconscious impulses toward the male partners in their life. The impulses can be negative or positive, and they're caused by an insufficient and/or complicated relationship with their fathers."

My brother, Chris, was born in June 1972 and we spent the next five years living in Kent, Washington, a suburb of Seattle. Our white house on 4th Avenue had peeling paint and tall evergreens on each side of the front porch. The scent of those trees was like pungent cat piss, something I wish I did not remember! We had a swing set in the backyard and a plastic pool that left rings of dead grass on the lawn. That is all I remember from that house, but the following story is one of many I have heard over the years since.

One evening, I fell from the monkey bars and crawled into the house to get help. Mom and Dad didn't think my injury was that bad, but my grandparents, who were there to play cards, argued that I needed to see a doctor. After I turned white, it became obvious it was time to go to the ER, where I was diagnosed with a broken arm. My grandparents had been right. They were always there to save me.

I spent my early years as an unofficial restaurant mascot, keeping myself entertained while my parents worked as a cook and a waitress. My dad's parents owned the Blue Candle, a diner with a dark, smoky cocktail lounge.

My mom is the youngest child in her family. Her grit is a direct reflection of being the little sister of three older brothers who taught her to hold her ground while being tormented.

When I turned seven, my dad decided to enroll at the Nazarene Seminary in Kansas, so we packed up and headed east. Two of my uncles relocated to Alaska to start a construction business around the same time. It tore my grandparents up when their little girl left for tornado land. Oh, Dorothy!!

"Monsters don't sleep under your bed; they sleep inside your head."
—Skylar Blue

The Groundbreaking News

When I turned ten, my parents sat me down and told me some shocking news: I was *adopted*! The details are fuzzy, and at the time, I didn't fully grasp what they were saying.

She feels completely confused and too young to understand what this means. She loves her mom and is close to her, but not to her dad. How could someone not want their child? Her young heart cracks open. As she tries to go to sleep that night, she questions everything.

The morning following this traumatic news, my mom could sense I did not comprehend the entire situation. We revisited the topic, and she explained in more detail that she *was* my biological mother, but "Dad" was not my biological father. Looking back, the news almost felt like it should have been obvious. My brother, Chris and I don't look alike, at all! I just never thought much of it as a kid, chalking it up to being normal sibling differences. He is tall and lanky, while I am the complete opposite, like Bert & Ernie from *Sesame Street* is how I would describe it. After that conversation, a lot of things suddenly made more sense.

Chris gave me a new nickname, "Little Orphan Angie," and started to act like quite the jokester, becoming a little brat to his big sister. I didn't have curly red hair like Orphan Annie, but I did have very pale skin and light-colored eyes, another characteristic that didn't match anyone in my immediate family.

Growing up, I was always one of those kids who was afraid to get in trouble. I feared my parents and hated to disappoint them. I was trying to gain approval in a house where expectations seemed high. My dad had control and anger issues.

One time, mom bought Frosted Flakes to make cookies. She had some cereal left over, so my brother and I ate it. Sugar-coated cereal was one of the foods we were not allowed to eat, according to my dad. Therefore, he punched the fridge and broke his hand. Served him right! His controlling ways would show up over the dumbest things — tiny, insignificant moments that turned into power plays.

Each evening, before bed, we were instructed to unlace his polished Oxfords and take them off. "Pull the heel first, and then the top," were his words, which still replay in my head. Then, his socks, which, of course, did not smell good.

The final reminder of who was in control was always the changing of the TV channel before walking up the stairs. There were no remotes back then, and God forbid our dad had to get out of his recliner. He was also a notorious sleepwalker, often roaming the house in the middle of the night, eyes open and mumbling nonsense while he paced the halls. One time, he was even holding a gun!

I felt like my dad was a ticking time bomb—we never knew what his mood would be... awake or asleep.

Boy, Oh Boy!

In elementary school, I enjoyed collecting stickers. My prized possession was a big, white photo album with stock paper, bound by brass tacks and filled with pages of stickers that I received as gifts or purchased with my allowance.

When I was in fourth grade, a boy in my class also had a huge collection of stickers, including some I had my eye on, and I had some he was after. Therefore, he became my first boyfriend! Were we going steady? No. Were we even dating? Well, no—I still was just a child. But my need to be wanted started at a young age, long before I understood the complexities of what it truly meant to belong. It was always there, quietly driving me to seek approval and love wherever I could find it. And that boy was gone as quickly as the other men in my life.

Growing up with a brother, I was surrounded by him and his friends, so, before I knew it, I turned into a tomboy, defined as "a girl who enjoys rough, noisy activities traditionally associated with boys." By contrast, normal girls were whinny and didn't like to get dirty.

They'd rope me into their games, which included playing Army (I was always the nurse), throwing the football, riding bikes, and being in a pretend band. We grabbed whatever makeshift instruments we could find—broomsticks for guitars, pots and pans for drums, plus my flute from band class. We choreographed ridiculous songs. For instance- "Grandpa's Hearing Aid," referring to the tiny hearing-aid batteries we'd found after my grandparents visited. This song was a top hit... in our bedroom and our minds. Being a tomboy allowed me to get attention from boys without having to give anything away. I didn't like the pressure of fitting into any traditional expectations of how girls were supposed to act.

When fifth grade started, so did those uncomfortable school video presentations about puberty, periods, and parts. *Vagina* and *penis* were foreign words to me before then. A week before the screenings in class, the little brown-paper sack of sanitary napkins was sent home, plus pamphlets to review, to prep us for the awkward video.

Thankfully, the girls had a different movie shown in a separate room. I can't imagine watching this movie around boys—creepy! *We bleed from where we pee?* So many unanswered questions. It seemed we were supposed to understand and not ask any questions, since the teachers looked just as uneasy as we did.

In the same year I became aware of the adoption, my parents told us they were splitting up. I took that news much easier than being adopted, maybe because of the lack of connection I felt with my "dad." Like most kids with divorced parents, we would have to go stay with him every other weekend. Unfortunately, he was nothing like a "Disneyland Dad," who indulges their kids with gifts and good times at their house, while Mom is left with all the discipline.

The only "gifts" we got at our dad's were overcooked fried hamburgers and a couch to sleep on in the basement of someone's house he had rented in a horrible part of town. He later moved to Texas, and we slowly started to hear from him less and less. What still sticks in my head, though, are memories of his controlling ways, even though I haven't seen or talked to him in decades.

My mom was now single, and for years to come, it was just the three of us—no father, no stepdad, no boyfriend.

I started my period that summer, when I was eleven. Thank God I had seen that video in school! My grandmother was the lucky person who got to explain the spots in my underwear. Then, we called my mom to tell her the news of Aunt Flo arriving. She cried. I assumed she felt bad for not being there during this "big" moment of my life.

Grandma Della always made things better, even my first period. She didn't make a big deal of it or act like it was something to be ashamed of. Instead, she just wrapped me in a big hug and reassured me that it was a part of becoming a woman.

By the time sixth grade began, I was prepared for this new monthly visitor, armed with pads in my little purse. You could always pick out who had "started" by what they carried to the bathroom. Quickly, boys figured out our little secret, and we could hear chuckles each time we headed to the girl's room, which left us feeling humiliated.

When my period came, so did the boobs, stretch marks, and long legs. I quickly grew to 5'3" and a size-C bra. While most of my friends were still playing with dolls, I was suddenly dealing with body changes and hormones that left me feeling out of sync. I realized I was way ahead of the puberty game when I became the center of attention, and Dolly Parton, Jr. ended up as my new nickname in the neighborhood and at school. I was being labeled once again.

The stares lingered a little longer, and the teasing took on a new tone. Part of me liked the attention but another part of me was deeply uncomfortable. I was still a kid but had to carry this added weight of being seen as something more—someone who appeared older and sexual long before I was ready.

My attention turned to a tall, blond, athletic boy many of my girlfriends admired. He lived in my neighborhood, and we had played together growing up. But, once puberty arrived, my reasons for liking boys shifted. I'm not insinuating I wanted to have sex with him, but I didn't consider him a childhood playmate anymore.

About this time my mom made a new rule, that my brother wasn't allowed to have his friends spend the night unless I was staying over at a friend's house. No big explanation, just a change I didn't understand at the time, but now makes perfect sense.

Our class planned a visit to Worlds of Fun, a big amusement park in Kansas City. This was an annual field trip for sixth graders before we ventured off to junior high. Once we arrived, we were set free for the day to ride roller coasters, eat carnival-type food, and hang out with friends.

It excited me to be free, but I had a different agenda than most of my friends. The cute boy from school was my focus. He liked the Philadelphia Phillies baseball team, so my mission that day was to tell him I liked him without verbally doing so. I found a store in the park that sold MLB fan merch, and I purchased a team batting hat to show my interest in the team and him. Then, once I had it, I spent the day searching for him, instead of enjoying my day with friends.

The gift worked... briefly. In elementary lingo, we started "going steady," but that ended just as quickly as it began, and I was left with the deeply ingrained sense of being unwanted.

> *She realizes that stickers and her looks aren't enough to keep the boys interested. She needs a tool to reel them in for longer. This emerging Monster keeps her from friendships she needs. Her identity starts to form, but it becomes attached to the desire to be accepted.*

My junior high school was adjacent to the elementary school, so my classmates made the journey to seventh grade with me. After the first quarter, my family moved to the westside of town, meaning I had to switch schools.

I wasn't upset we were making a change, because I had grown bored of the same old friends I'd grown up with. To me, this would be the fresh start I needed to forget those boys who had broken my heart. It was time for me to grow beyond the borders of who I used to be.

We moved into a duplex on a cul-de-sac, not far from school. When the weather allowed, I walked to school, which gave me the freedom to have fun on my terms without the watchful eyes of my mom or my brother. Thankfully, my grades were good with little effort, so I had plenty of time left to focus on other things: my social life.

I showed way more interest in spreading my butterfly wings than appeasing the school system. Softball was a sport I had started to play in fifth grade, but by the time I turned thirteen and was in eighth grade, I had no interest in an extracurricular sport. I only had eyes for boys—not textbooks and tests.

The football games, track meets, and baseball diamonds became a great place for me and my girlfriends to discover new fish in the sea. I developed many platonic relationships with guys I met, so I'm sure my mom didn't think twice when I started spending more time with some of the boys. Little did she know, I'd started dating them. If I didn't tell her, I wouldn't have to hear a lecture or, worse, her disappointment if she learned I was venturing into that territory.

The boys who didn't interest me were ones who appeared to be smart, too nice, or not tough enough. I liked them rough around the edges with a little fight in them. While I was seeking out the acceptance of boys, I had to skirt around my mom and her approval. I became very sneaky and smart when it came to spending time with boys. The secret added to the excitement.

My pen is stuck in the mud of shame as I enter the next part about the Men Monster saga. I think it occurred when I turned fourteen years old. My need for approval from a boy now meant having sex. My mom had no idea, however: I appeared way too young to be promiscuous. *Wink, wink.*

> *Different boys' images flash through her mind, with details foggy. She is filled with shame, which shuts out the memories of who she slept with first. Is she the only one who does such dirty things? What do they call "her" now? Having a boyfriend means she feels accepted, not alone, and safe from the other Monsters, so this becomes the space she feels the best in.*

FINDING HER

My first long-term boyfriend came from our circle of friends, someone I had known for a few years. Brad and I dated for over a year, and we were nominated Valentine King and Queen. Sadly, we weren't crowned, as our attire was not the norm. We rocked black-and-white punk outfits straight from the infamous Merry-Go-Round store at the local mall—because nothing says romance like a studded neck collar and parachute pants. Forget the fluffy dress and tux! I'm about as girly as a parka in an island paradise.

After that breakup, I began dating around. I did sleep with some of the guys, and we did use condoms… on occasion. *Phew!* I am so lucky I didn't end up pregnant. Abortion was not an option for me: it was expressly forbidden by my mom, and she had planted that seed long, long ago.

When my girlfriends started having the same unprotected sex, I saw the fallout of what an abortion did to many of my friends. Most of the time, doing so was followed inevitably by a breakup, which sent them into a deeper state of sadness. I did support them in their decisions, though. Who was I to say, *at that age*, what equaled right or wrong.

My friends and I regularly lied to our parents, often pretending we were staying at one house when, in reality, we were somewhere else entirely—maybe with a boy or just at another house that had fewer boundaries. It became a routine of sneaking around and sneaking out. It didn't take my mom long to figure that scheme out, though. Due to my newfound deceptive ways, before I could go spend the night with anyone, my mom called and had a chat with their parents, to make sure we were not trying to pull another stunt. I was embarrassed by her calls, which it reinforced the feeling that I couldn't be trusted. That stung.

Dating around became monotonous, and eventually my focus shifted. At one point, I had thoughts of going to college and being a psychologist, but instead, I focused on the hunt for my forever guy: a possible future husband. This was the start, not just wanting, but pursing my dreams to be a young wife and mother. Mind you, I was only in ninth grade.

> *As the Men Monsters grow, a new beast starts to form. Alcohol makes its appearance early in my life. As inhibitions are lessened, she keeps quiet. It becomes a way for her to accept what she does, even though she knows it is wrong.*

Liking it Bad

As ninth grade came to an end and high school appeared on the horizon, a new boy arrived in our school. West Virginia is where he came from, and his accent was evidence of his roots.

With his pierced ear, long hair, and a rebellious attitude, this new boy turned many heads. And I now had a new challenge: this wild stallion.

I watched this guy get into fights, defy authority, and make girls cry. He had the balls to do things I had never even imagined, which of course attracted me to him more and more.

My persistence paid off. Once I landed this bucking horse, my goal became to tame him. I didn't even consider waiting to have sex with him, though. I knew, based on his past flings and the rumors around school, he would expect that of me. How would I get him to stay, if I didn't comply?

When we started high school that next fall, I knew, given his flirty nature, that his being among fresh meat could make him stray and slip out of my grasp at any time. So, I figured it was time for a new plan of action—tend to his likes and interests.

I had convinced myself that, if I lost him, I would also lose my dreams of being a young wife and mom. This was the only vision I could see for myself. Hot rods, pot, alcohol, and sex became my hobbies now. As I persisted in my endeavors to stay with him, my girlfriends were no longer my priority. And neither was I.

My friends grew weary of my lack of commitment to them, and honestly, I can't blame them. Over time, it became obvious that I only reached out when I needed a shoulder to cry on—usually after one of my regular arguments with him left me feeling empty and broken. It didn't matter how toxic our relationship was becoming or how much of myself I gave up, my agenda was permanently set in stone.

> *His inner struggles are filled with anger and resentment for things in his past, a world she knows little about. Who is she to judge? Sharing his past life does not interest him, and if she pursues with questions, she might drive him away. "Her" good intentions are quieted.*

Our relationship mirrored a big roller coaster with a lot of highs and lows—thrilling, unpredictable, and emotionally exhausting. The highs kept me hooked. One minute, we were deeply in love, and the next, we were calling it off and then back in love. I started to see the signs of distress, but I remained dedicated to him, convinced I was "in love."

I quickly realized that jealousy turned into a big monster for him, and he was becoming a hothead. If another guy looked at me for too long, a conflict happened. Many times, this became a scheduled fight off of school property. His fights weren't always about me, even though I would have relished being so important to him. No, they simply depicted his anger. In West Virginia, he had wrestled; his stocky build gave him an advantage when he fought. He could kick some serious ass! Honestly, I don't think he ever lost a fight. He was unbeatable and that had me falling for him even more. My reputation at school changed alongside his.

> *Down below, she raises her hand. "Pick me, pick me! Open your eyes!"*
>
> *Her warnings are ignored. Sadly, she denies "her" true self. She becomes an attachment to someone else's happiness. She thinks she could change him, and that is how she will occupy "her" time.*

One day, during a passing period, we were in line at the vending machines, and a guy cut in front of us. *Oh shit*, I thought. I had become hyperaware of things I said, and I kept him away from anything that sparked his temper. Similar to walking through a field of landmines, but this time, someone had stepped wrong.

Words were exchanged, and then a few punches were thrown. Prior to this altercation, I had purchased a Hostess cream-filled pastry called a Banana Flip. As others grabbed my boyfriend to restrain him, I held the other guy back.

He was a tall, skinny kid who appeared scared and was not strong. As I held his wrists, he looked down at me with demon eyes. I thought he might punch me.

Then, suddenly, I heard my boyfriend yell, "*You touch her, you're dead!*"

So, instead of letting him punch me, I took that cream-filled pastry and shoved it in his face. Suddenly, we were all being detained and marched down to the principal's office. I felt so embarrassed, but at least I didn't have whipped cream all over my face. The guys were kicked out of school, but luckily, I was not.

The principal said, "You aren't a troublemaker. I think he is rubbing off on you, and he is a bad influence." He was right.

I was grateful that the school didn't call my mom, since she was quite the dictator at home. I quietly vowed to stay out of trouble, which only meant being craftier about my lies.

> *She loves the attention but knows it is the wrong kind. She needs to avoid the drama and make it through her senior year. Her devotion to him becomes her top priority, as having a man by her side becomes a non-negotiable.*

My mom began dating my stepdad, and they were married my senior year of high school. Since he wasn't around during most of my formative years, he never became that firm fatherly figure. I was grateful for the fact that he didn't try to overstep his role, but I often wonder what life would have been like with him around earlier, as I grew up. They are still married, and I love him dearly.

As graduation approached, we were all making plans for our futures. Some of my friends were going off to big colleges and doing the dorm life or the sorority thing. Neither of those sounded fun to me. I knew my plan, and I was sticking to it: Wife and Mom!

My boyfriend attended a graduation party with another girl, as he remained the wild horse I obviously hadn't corralled, like I'd thought. I went to a different party with my girlfriends and tried to ignore his interest in someone else.

That evening summed up our high school relationship. I spent the night mentally conflicted about what to do instead of enjoying my last days with friends.

> *So many signs from her. She knows this relationship feels wrong. Then why does she persist? Love is all she wants. This relationship feeds the Men Monsters, meanwhile denial becomes a cohort. This force drives her into hiding.*

Bridezilla

Two weeks after graduation, I moved into an apartment with a girl I worked with. Thankfully, I was smart enough to realize that living with my boyfriend right away was a bad idea, but at the same time, I spent most of my time with him anyway.

That fall, I enrolled in classes at the local community college while I worked as a waitress. My boyfriend wasn't sure of his plans, but marriage was not what he had in mind. I had it all figured out in my head until, one day, he surprised me by announcing he had enlisted in the Army!

What? You didn't even talk to me?

FINDING HER

The man I had invested so much time and love into was leaving me without hesitation! That was *not* my plan! The moment he signed those papers, the image I'd had for our future was shattered.

Clearly, he didn't need me like I needed him. There was no Woman Monster in his life, even though he probably thought I turned into a beast at times, while I kept my death grip on him.

Looking back, I respect him for taking such a scary leap, something I would never have done. I thought the military would change him. That, somehow, the discipline, the structure, and the rules would straighten out the wild edges I'd been trying to smooth for years.

As his enlistment date approached, the uncertainty of our future did, as well. The man I had worked so hard to keep just left. He started bootcamp in April and wouldn't return until October, then he'd be assigned to an unknown duty station for three years.

This turned out to be the first time I was solo since eighth grade. It felt lonely, and I didn't know how to reconnect with friends. The reality of bridges I burned in the past haunted me.

> *He has consumed her life, and now she feels like a stranger in the mirror. The silence seems unfamiliar and scary. She has been used to constant conversation and fighting. Now, there is time to sit and think. Maybe she will see the signs more clearly. Hopefully, this will be the time she listens to her.*

I filled my days with work and school. My new goal was to save money so we could get married when he completed his training. I couldn't focus: my grades were slipping and so was my desire to show up to class. My mom had agreed to pay for school if I kept a C average, which, in the past hadn't been a problem for me, but things were different now. My brain was consumed which left no room for learning at school. Since I couldn't make my grades, I had to pay my mom back for my tuition, which really put a hit on my pocketbook.

After he completed bootcamp, I took a trip to Oklahoma with his family to see him graduate. I made a T-shirt that read, *I Love my Soldier*. I was so proud of him and couldn't wait to see how he had changed, both physically and mentally.

I discovered he had transformed into someone completely different. I grew attracted to him more than ever! But my excitement stopped when he started to ask questions about my loyalty, while he was training far away. I blew that off, though, as I didn't want to ruin our day. We were able to spend that night together, and then he had to leave me again the next morning.

He spent the next four months in his military job training, and we were able to communicate on a regular basis. But then, his green-eyed monster exposed itself tenfold. He started to question literally everything I did and who I hung out with. Even though it upset me, it also brought on a sense of comfort, because, to me, it meant he truly cared.

Can you believe the denial I lived in?

> *She begins to find comfort in her moments of solitude, but this sense of peace is soon overshadowed by guilt, as if taking time for herself is an act of selfishness. Why doesn't she use this time to break it off? Her family and friends can see this*

Monster. She persists without listening to her, because love causes deafness.

That summer, I convinced him to ask me to be his wife. I know, crazy! I was hoping to calm all the questions he had regarding my whereabouts while he was away. I had grown sick of waiting, anyway, and knew this needed to happen as soon as he was assigned to a duty station, so I could go with him.

All of this transpired over the phone, not even in person. When he had a long weekend of leave, he came home for a quick visit and gave me a ring. It was nothing romantic, and I can't even remember the ring or anything else about that day. Maybe I can't recall those details because I would need to confront how much I'd hoped it would work, even though, deep down, I knew different.

As he began his training in another state, I stayed home, planning our wedding. The budget my parents gave me for the wedding wasn't enormous, so I had to get creative with the plans for our big day. I bought a fairy-tale-princess dress with layers of tulle that was on clearance. He would wear his military dress greens, which would cost us nothing, since the military had already issued them to him.

I was showered with all the new-home essentials and made ready for my soldier to come back and start our lives as husband and wife. My parents' new home was the perfect place for us to get married, since we were not members of any church. The big floor-to-ceiling windows provided a beautiful backdrop for our special day and we placed some furniture in rows to resemble pews in a church. My grandparents and cousins even planned to fly in to help.

As his homecoming drew closer, my excitement really began to grow. But then… it was delayed. His final schooling, which was airborne parachute training, was rescheduled due to Hurricane Hugo. I started to feel frantic, as you can imagine—Bridezilla!

She worries that this is another sign, but everything is set to go, and she can't cancel now. She is going to be a wife. Her thoughts are consumed with the future.

The day before the wedding, my soon-to-be husband finally arrived just in time to have a quick rehearsal. We were married on Friday, October 6, 1989, and the reception afterward was at a local community center. We were not even old enough to legally drink—but, of course, that didn't stop us.

As my dream of becoming a young wife was finally coming true, so were the harsh realities of our upcoming move. Leaving behind everything I had ever known was both thrilling and terrifying. The weekend before our relocation was nothing short of a whirlwind. We were married on Friday—with no honeymoon to follow. Saturday was spent cleaning the reception hall and my mom's house. On Sunday, we opened our wedding gifts. Monday, we picked up the U-Haul, and by Tuesday morning, we were saying goodbye to our families and everything we'd known.

There was so much hope and love that weekend, but also an ache in my chest that I couldn't quite figure out. It was the feeling of being young and brave, like jumping before knowing where you'll land.

Other than our move to Kansas when I was seven, and then visiting my grandparents back in Washington, I had not gone on a vacation or otherwise traveled, so this new adventure was over-the-top exciting! Our destination: Fort Bragg, North Carolina. This was where we would spend our first few years of marriage.

There are pictures my mom took of us standing next to the U-Haul, with the red hotrod in tow. We were nineteen years old and looked like little kids. But we packed up and headed east—just as my parents had done a decade before.

As I watched the countryside roll past, I daydreamed about our new surroundings. In my mind, this move--this fresh start—was the spark we needed to launch our marriage in the right direction. The distance from everything familiar seemed like the perfect reset.

> *She is excited and scared of what lies ahead. Will he be tamed after the military training? Her persistence has paid off, and she is more confident than ever that she can make this work. It has to. They are tied by a vow, and there is no turning back.*

There was no way I was living in military housing. Too many rules for me. Also, I felt some resentment toward the Army, because it had taken him away from me earlier that year. We settled in a mobile home park outside of the Army base, which was all we could afford.

Our community was filled with other young couples just like us. I was now a military wife, though I did not truly know what that entailed. Our tiny two-bedroom, one-bath, hallway-like home was perfect. I can still visualize the dark-blue and mauve felt upholstery that covered the sofa and chair we purchased on a payment plan. These were easy to come by in a military town.

Since we only had his 1972 Chevy Chevelle, I took him to the Army base on days I needed a car. I never liked the feeling of being tied down to the house, and I needed a purpose beyond the routine of laundry, dishes, and waiting for the day to pass. So, I began to search for a job. My past waitressing skills were useful for getting hired at a restaurant by the mall. Soon, we purchased a new car, and we began to settle into military life.

It was common for the wives to stay behind while their husbands did field training. Sometimes, I would be left alone for day or weeks. Thankfully, we became friends with our neighbors, so I had a girlfriend to keep me company while the men were away. When the guys were home, our weekends were spent playing cards, drinking beer, and smoking cigarettes.

The green-eyed Jealousy Monster was not gone, however, as I'd originally hoped it would be. I'd made the assumption that things would be different, now that he had strict military training, but I was wrong once again.

My manager at work made a pass at me. He cornered me in the walk-in cooler and tried to kiss me. I pushed him away and ran out. I felt small and powerless, like my worth was being measured by something that had nothing to do with my work ethic. I questioned myself. Was it really that big of a deal? Did I do something wrong?

The job I'd once loved became a place I dreaded going to, but I never told my husband, as I feared his reaction and the scene he might cause. Sadly, I was also afraid he would blame me for what happened.

Back home, my mom made bets I would be pregnant within a year of being married. Guess what? She happened to be right, again!

> *Her mom seems to know her better than she does. Or could it be because she doesn't want to know who she has become? Her mom's opinions become something she doesn't ask for, as she doesn't want to hear any opposition to decisions she's making.*

In June 1990, only one month after stopping birth control, I took a pregnancy test and saw the two red lines. Can you say Fertile Myrtle? Upon the news of our family growing, we moved to an adorable three-bedroom, one-bath home across the street from our trailer park. It had a garage in the back that proved great for his hot-rod tinkering, plus it had a pond for fishing. Large pine trees shaded the house, which had been newly renovated. It felt like we had built a new beginning. I loved this little house in the pines.

As we were celebrating the news of our new baby coming, we weren't aware of the trouble brewing overseas.

Braving the Storm Alone

I can vividly remember that hot, humid summer evening when we were coerced into attending a presentation at the Shoney's Big Boy restaurant. Little did we know, it was an Amway meeting!

While the guy up front showed us the millions of dollars we could make, people around the room were getting messages on their pagers, instructing them to call their unit commanders. As a military wife, we had been warned about these situations, but nothing can really prepare you for the moment it happens.

Desert Storm was mobilizing soldiers and deploying them to Iraq. In my head, I kept ruminating, *This can't be happening! This wasn't part of my plan. I am two months pregnant. No, no, no!*

We rushed home, where he packed his things, and then I drove him to the base. He left U.S. soil the second week of August. At twenty years old, I found myself alone and pregnant in a town with no other family and suddenly faced with the overwhelming weight of two lives: mine and the one growing inside.

My friend's husband wasn't deployed with mine, so I became their third wheel. I desperately needed the support and a distraction from the television and the news of what was happening in Iraq. When I didn't think things could get any worse, they did. After babysitting for my friend's baby, I returned home to find our house had been broken into.

The back door was slightly open, and the lock had been jimmied. I phoned the police and waited in the car. Thankfully, the thieves only took stereo equipment, but it left me feeling violated. The detectives covered my house with black dust to find any fingerprints, then they filed the report and left. Sadly, robberies were running rampant in our area, due to so many women being home alone.

Immediately, I called my friend to come pick me up. I was so scared that they would come back that night to steal more. My friend and I must have looked ridiculous as we shoved a mattress into the back seat of her compact car. But there was no way I could stay there at my house one more night. The next day, I booked a flight back to Kansas, where

FINDING HER

I would stay until my soldier came home. Little did I know that would be the next year.

> *Just as quickly as her life as a wife and soon to be mother comes together, it is being torn apart. For the first time, she feels sick to her stomach, not from morning sickness but at the thought of what could happen to her soldier. As reality sets in, she knows she has to be strong for him and, now, for this baby.*

Letters with photos and the occasional phone call were the only communication from him over the next nine months. My eyes remained glued to the TV, as that was the best way for me to get updates on when this nightmare would be over.

His green-eyed jealousy monster emerged again, even though we were countries apart and I was carrying his child. When his calls came in from the sandbox, they always included questions about my faithfulness. The deployment was a nightmare for me and many other families, and this only made things worse.

> *Her self-worth, as a pregnant wife, has been damaged. She can't understand how he can even think she is doing something so awful. This Men Monster starts to take control of her again. Why does she let it? She forces the feelings of sadness deep down, quieting herself once again.*

As the days dragged on and on, there was no sign of my husband returning home before the baby came. I stayed in Kansas to have the baby, and my mom would be my labor and delivery coach. She stepped in without hesitation, like she always has, even when I have been too scared to ask for help. In that delivery room, with all the fear, pain and anxiety, she was my savior!

My beautiful baby girl was born March 14, 1991 after twenty-four hours of labor. I believe Megan was trying to wait as long as she could to come out. She wanted her daddy there, and so did I.

When Megan was eighteen days old, he returned home from the war. Happy days ahead!

As we settled into being a family of three, I looked forward to his enlistment coming to an end the following year. I think he really wanted to reenlist, but after what I had endured, there was no way I would be a military wife any longer than I had to.

The baby's well-being was now her priority. Her voice emerges and is strong whenever it concerns this little girl. She feels as if she's walking in heaven when she becomes a mom, and no Monsters can take that from her.

"Men may fight the battle, but women wage the war."
—Katlyn Charlesworth, *The Patriot's Daughter*

Stomping Grounds

We had never lived in our hometown as a married couple before, so now, there were new, unfamiliar influences on our marriage. Since the green-eyed monster hadn't disappeared when I was pregnant, why would I think it would go away when we were back home? I thought we could navigate this change together. We had made it through the war together, through distance, uncertainty, and days filled with worry. So, this we could do.

A year later, we purchased our first home. Along with that came the news of baby number two. It only took a couple of months to get pregnant—Fertile Myrtle *again*!

Of course, we argued after finding out. He felt blindsided, like I had made a major decision without him—which was not true! We'd discussed having another baby, and I went off the pill, but he didn't see it that way. His mistrust of me only deepened after that.

> *Her hormonal spirits are dampened. She despises being confronted, as it makes her question her true intentions. As the conflict grows within, she settles back into the abyss, while she grows another human inside. All she wants is happiness for herself and her baby.*

Our second beautiful baby girl, Lauren, came in August 1993. Our family felt complete!

During the time my husband spent in the Army, he qualified for the G.I. Bill, which helped pay for college. After our Lauren was born, he decided to pursue a degree in nursing. While I kept things settled on the home front, he followed his dreams. I had mine, so why couldn't he? Or did I?

I was a stay-at-home mom during the day and a bartender by night. This gave us the flexibility to keep our girls out of daycare while providing the family some income. He applied to nursing school and was accepted.

Our lives were going somewhere, but it felt like we were on different paths. I found myself growing proud of him even though, deep down, our marriage was a mess. My focus shifted entirely to family—the girls and the house.

Meanwhile, his attention was on himself—his goals and his needs. I became jealous and resentful.

> *She thinks about her life and what it will look like in the future. She can't even imagine what she wants to be, besides a wife and mom. She has cornered herself into an identity dictated by others. That is easier than finding her.*

As his school schedule consumed more of his time and his ability to work lessened, I took on more of the household financial responsibilities. I had no desire to leave my girls with someone else during the day, so the best solution was to run a daycare in my house and work more at night. When he wasn't studying, he could be found in the garage or out with friends. I constantly felt like I had been put on a back burner. He seemed to have no time for me or his children.

> *She pushes those feelings aside, as it seems selfish for her to think he doesn't deserve his own time. She wonders if his new career path will change him. Will he be more attentive to the family, once he feels established in his new career? She doesn't know what she will do with her free time, so she shoves her deep inside, once again.*

While he continued pursuing of his career, the girls entered the school system, which allowed me more free time. I enjoyed working at the bar, so I took on extra shifts. The attention I received from customers, positive or negative, helped fill both my cup and our bank account.

I was a great bartender and a good ear for those who needed free therapy. But I didn't realize that I was the one who needed it more. The resentment toward him grew, along with our other mounting marital problems.

Split Decision

Our marriage was hanging by a thread. Over the years, I had suggested counseling, but his macho personality wouldn't allow for his feelings to be divulged to a stranger.

Together, we made the tough decision to separate while we tried to work things out. There were no formal court filings, for now. We hoped we could address the situation without spending money on attorneys and court fees. Plus, if we filed, it would be a public record and published in the local newspaper. It's not like we did not tell anyone, but this way felt less official, and I hoped this would put us on the path to a happy marriage. We were young, dumb, and in love—or so I thought!

I stayed in our home, and he moved in with a friend. When it became his weekend to have the girls, I would work extra hours, because being alone brought back memories of the war, and the solitude felt painful.

The regulars at the bar became part of my extended family. They also were accustomed to visits from my girls and the jealous husband. Those days, the therapy roles at the bar were reversed. My customers were consoling me.

When I realized I would be a single mom and needed a better job, it forced me to explore other options. The house felt less stressful once he left and I began to gain control.

Real estate was the path I chose, for the time being. I absolutely loved houses and creating spaces to make them feel like a home. The people skills I had gained from working at the bar seemed perfect for this new role. I went to school, passed my exam, got my real estate license, and found an office that would take me on as a new agent.

While I tried to make this new career work, I continued to work random shifts at the bar. Real estate takes time to build a customer base, and patience is not a virtue this girl possesses. Meanwhile, he had started to work in a hospital for his clinicals and quickly found other women who interested him. I did the same thing at my bar.

We were both playing the field—not even divorced, and yet searching for the next one.

> *She knows nothing about what qualities she likes in a man, and dating is a completely unfamiliar experience to her. Why can't she simply be with herself? Is it too painful? Being alone is scary. The Alcohol Monster is beginning to make more appearances in her life, while she enjoys the kid-free weekends.*

I thought I would never be the one to cheat, but we were both doing it while we were still legally married. One of my flings was a customer who took interest in me. He was married, and I knew it.

One day, fling #1 and I met in a parking lot. I got into his car, and we drove to his house. His wife was at work. As we entered his neighborhood, I was instructed to duck down and hide this deception. He opened the garage, pulled the car in, and shut the door. Then, we went upstairs. I can't remember many of the details, except for the song that played while we had sex in his marital bed.

I thought he really wanted to be with me, but I quickly realized that was not the case. He denied my phone calls and acted like he barely knew me, when he came to the bar.

> *What the hell is she thinking? Why is she so naive? The Monster attacks her from all angles. It goes against everything she stands for. The yearning for love is greater, and it*

overpowers her once again. She will do things outside the norm, just to feel worthy.

Next, it was a customer who also happened to be in real estate. He didn't treat me like the one before. He was divorced and had a daughter—perfect!

Even though I was still married, in my mind, we were done, and it was just a matter of paperwork to finalize the divorce. I introduced fling #2 to my girls, and we enjoyed each other's company for a while.

While she has new adventures to keep her busy, she still wonders if her husband had changed and if, maybe, they can work things out. That would be easier for her, since that is what she's wanted since she was a little girl. So consumed with these dreams, she doesn't allow time to discover her.

Let's Get it On

Things suddenly changed one Sunday evening, when my husband brought the girls back home after having them for the weekend.

For some reason, he decided to stay and help me put the girls to bed. After they'd been tucked away, we had a few beers. We talked, drank, cried, drank some more, and, yep—ended up in bed.

I'd missed him and his familiar touch. That evening, we consummated our marriage once again and decided to get back together. Of course, the girls were ecstatic to hear the news.

The Alcohol and Men Monsters are working together, and it proves to be a powerful partnership. She has a pit in her gut. Her voice tries to be heard. This isn't right, you know this. What are you doing? She quickly shuts her up by focusing on the matter at hand. That, as usual, is not her.

Once my life had started back on the right path, it was time to find a larger home, since the girls required more bathroom time, and the house we had wasn't going to cut it any longer. A new school and neighborhood would be another fresh start for our kids and our marriage.

We moved to a newly built house, but it proved to be a mistake. It backed up to the highway, therefore we grew tired of living there quickly. The constant noise and vibrations from traffic were enough to drive me to drink. Oh wait, I'm not to that chapter yet.

Next, we found an older, larger home down the street with a pool and beautiful mature trees. I loved the shade in the backyard, as well as the layout of this house. It had four levels, large rooms, plenty of space for all of us, and no annoying traffic! Decorating, wallpapering, and painting were the hobbies that kept me busy, while the girls enjoyed swimming with their friends.

It seemed like we were the Cleaver family—at least from the outside looking in. (If you don't know who that is, Leave it to Beaver was an old black-and-white television show about a family that seemed ridiculously perfect, though that name wouldn't work in these times. Ha-ha-ha!)

As life went on, the distance between us grew. We were growing apart. The once-reunited love became a distant memory, and once again, he started to spend more time away from the family. We had started playing together on a coed softball team, and after the games, the girls and I would go home, while he joined the team for food and drinks. I was not invited.

> *His jealousy disappears from their relationship, and she knows it could be a sign. She finally listens to herself and uses this little nudge to fuel her curiosity as to what had changed. He has always been a flirt, but this feels different. Is he seeing someone else? How can she walk away? So much has gotten better, while so much has grown worse. Her reasons for leaving don't seem adequate.*

The time my husband was away he didn't always spend with the opposite sex. He'd head out with friends, doing things he never cared about before, like cave exploring. It wasn't that he was just out there without me. It was the fact that we had never shared any of these types of activities together. He'd come back a little livelier and more fulfilled, which felt like a slap in the face... Oh, wait. It was!

When he returned home from a weekend exploring with a friend, we had a fight, and I decided poke the bear.

To purposely provoke him, I asked, "Are you in love with your friend and is that why you're spending so much time with him?"

I knew he wasn't interested in other men, but I had no other way to hurt him, except my nasty words. He slapped me! It happened so fast, I didn't even register it at first. While I was in shock, what hit the hardest was the realization that, for the first time, I didn't need to convince myself that things could change or I could make it work.

As I stool there, I knew. I finally had a reason to leave. It saddened me that it took a physical altercation for me to finally make that decision, but at the same time, I felt a weight had been lifted. Now, I had the right to walk away. And I did.

> *The Monsters aren't letting her go easily. She needs a big sign to leave, as her self-confidence has diminished during their last separation. She doesn't even feel worthy of a divorce. Until now.*

The altercation happened right before the holidays. My girls had experienced enough, so at least we could agree on one thing: wait to tell the girls after the first of the year. The girls knew about our troubles, and they were upstairs when the final blow came.

One thing I knew for sure, the girls and I were staying put, as I didn't want to move them during this chaotic time. I had recently reframed my thinking about divorce, and now, I wasn't staying for the kids—just the opposite. They didn't need to grow up with parents who weren't happy together. I was finally done!

> *She prepares for single-mom life, once again. Her anger about what he's done becomes the weapon she needs to fight this Monster, once and for all… But the Men Monsters are here to stay. They are destroying her on a deeper level. The place where shame, belittling, and losing sense of self happens. She isn't aware of any of this, since they are good at hiding and stay away when her intuition tries to be heard.*

Thankfully, during that difficult time, I crossed paths with a nice guy named Mark. He was a customer dealing with his own divorce. I suppose there was something about our shared heartaches that made our friendship grow.

He wasn't just a customer with a friendly face; he offered wisdom and advice that helped me process things in ways I hadn't been able to, on my own. Mark had different views on marriage and divorce, seeing things through a man's eyes, and he shared perspectives I hadn't considered before. We remained friends and lent each other an ear when needed. Our relationship was platonic at the time, and he eventually got engaged to a girl with whom I became friends.

The Dirty Dating Pool and Number Two

The divorce was finalized a year later, and I settled into my new routine. I was now back to fishing in the sea at the age of twenty-eight.

Dating websites were starting up, and I tried that a time or two with very bad luck. One guy was a cocaine user. Another stalked me after one date, by sending letters to my work when I ignored his calls. I am so lucky I wasn't killed, as my common sense had gone out the window!

My search for the right man continued. One female customer I had become friends with introduced me to her new roommate. He was average height, with a stocky build and dark hair... my usual preferences. His laid-back personality lured me in, along with a bigger bonus: no baggage—no kids or wife.

Let's call him the Rebound Monster. If you look up the definition of a "rebound relationship," it explains that 1,000,000%:

> *A romantic partnership that begins shortly after ending a previous relationship, where a person enters a new connection before fully healing from the emotional wounds of the past breakup, often using the new partner as a distraction or to avoid dealing with their pain. Essentially, it's a relationship started as a reaction to a recent heartbreak, rather than genuine feelings for the new partner. These relationships can move quickly due to the desire to fill the void left by the previous relationship. While not always detrimental, rebound relationships can be damaging if they prevent proper emotional healing.*

I learned later that my friend had found this roommate from a Craigslist ad. If I had only known this important fact, things might have been different.

Nah, who am I kidding? I know myself better than that.

He took me on real dates, something I had not been accustomed to. He picked me up, took me out to dinner, and he even paid! But romancing me became his tool to trap me. My blinders continued to be on, and, sadly, my girls could see things way better than I could. Was I drifting through life with my eyes wide shut?

> *She feels like a princess. Never in her life has she been treated so well. Any clues from within are blinded by the facade of this Prince Charming.*

He surprised me one day by showing up at my work and telling me that one of his customers had a hot-air balloon, and we were going for a ride. *How cool,* I thought.

We set out on a breathtaking flight over the city. As the balloon started to descend over a football field, he handed me binoculars and said, "What does that sign down there say?"

I pressed my eyes against the binoculars and pointed them toward the field. There, printed out in huge letters were the words: *WILL YOU MARRY ME?*

I couldn't believe what I was seeing. I turned to him just as he opened a box and put a ring on my finger. Of course, I said, "Yes!" This is what little girls dream of. The fairy tale engagement I didn't have, the last go round!

Oh wait, it gets better... When we arrived back at the house to tell the girls, I noticed a bunch of cars on our street. He had planned an engagement party, with food and all. My parents and girls were there, too, but everyone had quiet concerns, since we had only been dating for six months.

He had every detail figured out; he'd even spoken to my boss before picking me up that afternoon. No one had ever done so much for me. I was in love!

Honestly, I don't even remember the actual date of our wedding. Some things are better left in the dark recesses of memory. We had a formal church wedding, followed by a reception at the local community center—the same place where my first one transpired. The place was cheap, and everyone knew where it was located, so why not?

It didn't take long for me to realize that this whole thing covered up who he really was. I had always considered myself a good judge of character. This became a skill I'd gained from my interactions and observations in the service industry. Over the next two years, his personality changed, and I began to hear conflicting stories about his past.

> *She starts to see the real Monster but can't see the partnership that develops, waiting for the perfect time to strike. The Men and Money Monsters will be the Wonder Twins and shove her into the abyss.*

First, Rebound Hubby lost his job. We were broke (more on that coming soon), and it became apparent it was time for me to leave him.

Even though I left, he kept control over me through his deceptive ways. After I told him I was moving out, he put my stuff on the curb and changed the locks. He also took a picture collage I had made of me and my girls and replaced each photo with those of just him and me. Creepy!

I grew scared of him. He knew some sketchy people from his connections at the golf course. Big Mafia types who would do favors for people... No kidding!

My mom lived close by, and she welcomed us with open arms. While we were living there, he wrote long letters and put them in her mailbox at the bottom of her driveway. I told him to stay away or I would get a restraining order. He would simply laugh.

Then, seemingly out of nowhere, he claimed he had cancer. It felt less like a revelation and more like a desperate attempt to pull me back in. Of course, the timing was suspicious, and deep down I knew this was a manipulative ploy rather than a genuine health crisis. It wasn't about illness—it was about control, reeling me in when he knew I was slipping away.

Then, he told me he wanted to have a baby with me. *He was crazy!* The final drama was his suicide attempt... Or let's just say, his last attempt to grab my attention.

He called some friends while he was drunk and conveyed some weird things. Then, he checked into a casino hotel room. No one could find him or reach him via phone. He wouldn't answer. One of his friends contacted the police, and once they found his location, they had the hotel staff open the door and found him inside. They also discovered my wedding ring, a credit card, bullets, and beer cans all over the hotel room.

The police took him into custody, and it felt like something straight out of a nightmare. I couldn't comprehend how I could have missed his alt-personality. There were so many things I didn't know. They took him to a local hospital: not a jail cell, but to the mental-health floor.

After a few days of observation, they allowed him to make a phone call, and he tried to convince me to come see him. Promises of his sanity and excuses of it being a big misunderstanding poured from his lying mouth… blah, blah, blah, blah, blah.

"Rot in hell!" I told him. Honestly, I wished him dead.

Now broke and broken, I left with nothing but a few possessions and another failed marriage. *What was my problem?*

Jokes were now commonplace amongst my family and friends. "She gets a new man, a new house, and her new car every year." I wasn't laughing.

I was ashamed, embarrassed, and questioned everything, not just about him but about myself. I had lost it all, which almost included the custody of my girls when he threatened to lie to my ex-husband about me and get them taken away. Royal piece of shit!

He never showed up for any of the divorce proceedings, and I have no idea where he is now. We were married for less than three years, and I wish I could erase all of them. The hurt he caused me is gone now. I chalked it up to a very hard lesson, but one I probably needed.

> *Why can't she be happy? She doesn't know how to live life alone. It is easier to fill the voids with Monsters than give her a chance to come forward.*

Third Time is a Charm

After twelve years working at the same bar, it was time to change the scenery. It also gave me an outlet for finding a new boyfriend.

I started a job at a cool new place, a Mexican cantina that turned into a dance/karaoke bar at night. It had the best frozen margaritas!

Over time, my relationship with my boss evolved, and we began dating. But thankfully, he turned out to be nothing like a monster. He was a nice guy—genuine, considerate, and kind in ways that made me feel safe and appreciated. As we continued to date, I realized I couldn't be with him long-term. This girl needed more pizzazz or wow factor, and he was so chill.

When I realized my boss wasn't going to be "the one," Mark, the customer I had met at my bar when I was dealing with my first divorce, broke off his engagement to his fiancée, a friend of mine. Well, *she* broke it off. We had all remained friends for the past ten years. Her abrupt breakup surprised our whole group of friends.

Mark reached out for support when he was dealing with this devastating event, and our platonic friendship continued to grow. The two of us had always gotten along whenever we'd taken group trips to Mexico, gone canoeing, or headed to the lake. He liked lots of activities and was funny—still is. He also had a great career, which meant he was financially responsible.

As I helped Mark get over his breakup, he assisted me in moving into a new rental house. One night, at a biker bar, he told a friend he'd wanted to kiss me for years, and, finally, he did.

Even though his job was stressful and required weird rotating shifts, we had no problem making time for dates. We enjoyed motorcycle rides to a patio for lunch, nights at home watching movies, and happy hour at the local watering hole—it didn't matter what we were doing, we were having fun, and he felt safe.

My girls had known Mark through our long friendship. They were fifteen and thirteen by then, and Mark's three kids were moving out soon. One month after that first kiss, as we returned home from a motorcycle ride, Mark asked me to be his wife.

My response was, "F***, yes!" while I was still wearing my leather chaps and jacket. I ran right upstairs to my girls' room to share the news, but they weren't impressed, as they had been here before.

> *She is happy, and they aren't. Deep inside, she understands, because these Monsters have already ruined part of their childhood. Even though she loves him, everyone will question her actions, since her track record has proven differently. She promises her this will be the last one, and she will make her proud.*

Our wedding followed the next February, but we couldn't wait to live together. I thought about the money we could save—I had been very budget-conscious as a single mom. Mark told me to find the perfect house, so I did. An amazing four-bedroom house on two wooded acres with a pool.

We moved in together in August and anxiously awaited our upcoming vows. Mark was different from the others in ways beyond the surface. With him, I could tell the difference in the way he looked at me, the way he treated me, and, most important, in the way he made me feel about myself. He loved me for who I was, flaws and all. Most of all, there was a trust in him that I had never known before. I knew I could count on him and didn't have to wonder whether he would cheat.

Happily Ever After

Fast forward almost twenty years, and here we are, still married. It hasn't always been perfect, but we've overcome every challenge that came our way and grew stronger and more united than ever. As you continue to read, I will share some of the things we have endured to get here.

> "How good and thoughtful he is; the world seems full of good men—
> even if there are monsters in it."
> —Bram Stoker

Monster 2

Money

LOSER AND *PIECE OF CRAP* were the words I would have used to describe anyone who claimed bankruptcy—until it happened to me.

Dollar Daze

As I write this, I am fifty-four years old, so I have been working for about forty years. Can you try to guess how many different jobs I have had? Well, if you guessed thirty, you'd be right! Don't worry, I am not going to tell you about each one.

I realized that the Money and Job Monsters were like bipolar beings, pulling me into two conflicting directions. They had consumed much of my life—they fueled my drive and pushed me to work harder, to secure a stable income, which made me feel like I was in a game of tug-of-war between success and emptiness.

When I was seven, we moved to Kansas for my dad to attend schooling to become a pastor in the Nazarene Church. We lived in a two-bedroom townhome in a government-subsidized community called Westerfeld

Place. There were rows of tall, skinny homes connected in groupings of ten with shared walls. We paid the rent we could afford based on our income, which wasn't much.

Dad's busy school schedule didn't allow him to work very much, so things were tight. Sound familiar? Mom got a job working as a bookkeeper, since numbers were always her specialty. She kept our ship afloat with a budget that involved spreadsheets and precise tracking. Still to this day, she keeps every receipt, balances her checking account, and blows me away with her Excel sheets.

I shared a room with bunk beds with my brother. On the one hand, it brought us closer together. But at the same time, the arguments over who got the top bunk became annoying, just like he did. He was my only friend until we settled into our new community and started making new ones.

Growing up, I had no clue we lived in a "poor" neighborhood, since I never felt as if I lacked for anything. It turned into a great place to live, though, as we had playgrounds, tennis courts, sidewalks, and bikes to ride. We spent our days outside, only coming home when called for dinner or the streetlights came on. It was a close-knit community, and everyone looked out for others.

My first memory of a job or money was as a child doing chores. As payment, we received a roof over our heads, food to eat, and clothes to wear. It was everyone's job to pitch in and earn your keep. Living wasn't free.

Of course, my brother and I felt like we were doing all the work, and we put the chores off as long as possible. Vacuuming, sweeping, dusting, and dishes were the ones I recall. I dreaded weekends when we had to clean our rooms from top to bottom, making them spick-and-span, with inspections afterward.

The Saturday morning rule was always: clean your room and then you can go play. It was that simple, but somehow, we made it complicated. I did discover, if I shoved my stuff into a box and hid it underneath the bed, I could get to the playground faster. The quicker I could complete this chore, the better. I was sneaky or, as I like to say, "creative" at an early age.

My social butterfly wings were starting to grow, and therefore, I really did not want to miss out on what was happening outside. Maybe there should be a FOMO monster in my book? (For those not familiar, FOMO means fear of missing out.)

Once my parents could afford it, my brother and I began receiving an allowance. One dollar a week, which we spent quickly at the local 7-Eleven convenience store. Slurpees were my favorite! Do you remember the Suicide Slurpee? You mixed all the flavors available on tap, which, typically, were cherry and cola. Damn, those things were good.

Other days, my purchases included Tootsie Roll Pops and Bubble Yum. Grape for me, please. The freedom to spend that dollar any way we desired made us feel like we had power over our financial decisions. There were no rules about saving it, so it was gone as soon as it landed in our hands. Also, the story of my adult life!

For our family, school lunches were provided at a discount. The "reduced lunch program" was the official name. Mom would send us to school with money that we would take to the office, and in return, we received a punch card. My card was a different color than the other kids', which signified I was in this program. As we lined up for lunch, we handed the lunch lady the card, so she could punch a hole in it. Thankfully, kids didn't bully others like they do now. I loved the brown-bag lunches we brought to school at times. Peanut butter and jelly sandwich, Doritos, and a banana were one of my favorites.

> *She lives in special housing and has different prices for her food at school, but she never feels poor. She doesn't know any other life. The Food and Money Monsters are collaborating inside her at an early age.*

After my parents divorced when I was ten, money was tighter than ever. I didn't feel the squeeze, but I am sure my mom did. She worked fifty hours a week, and during tax season, even more. I learned at an early age that taxes suck! Then, my mother decided to enroll in school to become a CPA (Certified Public Accountant). Those classes kept her busy in the evenings a few nights a week.

Garage sales were a way we could make extra money to do fun things like go to Chuck E. Cheese (called Showbiz Pizza back then). That place had creepy animated bears that clanged symbols and played songs. Also, Skee-Ball, arcade games, pizza and pop—a kid's dream.

Sadly, one of our garage sales ended with my brother slicing a part of his finger off, and all the money we earned went toward his medical bills, so there was no pizza fun that year. My brother and I still reminisce and argue over who's really to blame for what happened.

We were digging in the neighborhood dumpster, which was a pastime, to find cardboard boxes and such for fort-building. Well, that day, we found an unfamiliar treasure: an air filter with chicken-wire mesh on it. As we were tugging to see who would take possession, my brother cut his finger on the wire. It was his fault! That's my story, and I'm sticking to it! Sorry, bro.

When I was twelve, my mom bought a duplex, and we moved to the westside of town. The westside was known as "the wrong side of the tracks," but I didn't care, as we were finally free of the "poor house."

Off to Work I Go... Ho, Ho, Ho!

After turning thirteen, I started babysitting to earn and save money, since there still wasn't a ton of extra cash in our budget. The neighbor a few doors down had three boys, and she paid well!

I was responsible for funding my own desire for trendy clothes, and with driving on the horizon, I also needed to start saving for a car and insurance.

When I turned fifteen, my mom strategically used Wite-Out to change my date of birth on my certificate, so I could get my first real job. Hardee's, also known as Carl's Jr. on the West Coast, hired me for a whopping $3.05 an hour!

I was filled with a mix of excitement and nervousness, like I was on the brink of something big but didn't know what to expect. I was thrilled to be earning my own money but knew it would be gone as fast as it was earned.

Proudly, I wore brown polyester pants, an orange-plaid, short-sleeved button-up, and a stunning brown hat to serve burgers and fries. I still feel frumpy just visualizing how I must have looked.

I still remember "taking," probably more like stealing, their hot ham-and-cheese sandwiches, which I loved. Thank goodness for the large pockets in my brown polyester pants:

they were a perfect fit for those warm sandwiches. I would walk quickly to the bathroom and scarf down my lunch while I peed. Gross!

This is when I began my love for the food service industry. My people-pleasing demeanor and gift of gab turned out to be perfect for that environment. Plus, it gave me the chance to break free from home. Work was fun and rewarding.

> *As she ventures out into the world, she can see what others have and what she does not. It doesn't seem fair. A saying of her mom's repeats in her head, "Life isn't fair, and the quicker you realize it, the better." She has lots of energy, more than most people, which makes work effortless. Her value starts to be equated with the money she earns.*

After working at Hardee's for a year, I was now legal to work anywhere and could drive. Thanks to my grandparents giving me my first loan, I could afford a white, stick-shift Ford Fairmont with red vinyl seats and a sunroof. My first monthly payment and insurance meant I needed more money, so I searched for a waitressing job where I could make tips.

I found a job at an iconic burger place called Winstead's. They had the best burgers and onion rings, not to mention the special skyscraper malts for dipping our fries in. I'm getting hungry just thinking about it.

They had me wear another uniform that still makes me cringe. It was a light-green, one-piece dress with a dark-green apron and a mauve napkin folded to resemble a brooch pinned together with a gold miniature fork and knife. Thank goodness I wasn't tipped based on my attire!

> "Formal education will make you a living; self-education will make you a fortune."
> —Jim Rohn

Hidden Treasures

It didn't take me long to figure out that tips were like gold, and no one, not even my mom or the government, kept track of how much I made. It was the perfect system: the cash came in fast, and I felt free about the fact that I didn't have to report every dime. I was in control, and that instilled a sense of power.

The quick pace of "being in a rush" with the lunch or dinner crowd thrilled me. I despised the slow times, because they meant doing side work like rolling silverware or cleaning ketchup bottles, and there were no tips for those chores.

I quickly moved up the food chain. Get it…? Ha-ha! As a senior in high school, I became shift manager and trained the new staff. This was another task I enjoyed. If I was a good trainer and turned them into great servers, then people would come back, and, of course, that equated to more money for me.

Not everyone is cut out for this kind of work, but most people eventually realize that on their own and end up quitting. Firing people felt confrontational, which is not my strong suit. I wasn't built for conflict, and I hated disappointing anyone—even a new coworker.

After high school, I moved into an apartment and was able to afford anything I wanted, while I raked in the cash. I worked at Winstead's until I got married and moved to

North Carolina. It was easy to find a job in my new town, since I had three years in this industry under my belt.

By then, I had figured out what made a restaurant a gold mine: location, location, location. Rock-ola Café is where I landed. I lived in a military town, and this bar and grill sat right by the mall—score! Plus, it got me out of the house and gave me time to myself. I wasn't one to sit around and be unproductive.

Double shifts on Friday and Saturday were the way to make the big bucks. It wasn't glamourous, and it certainly wasn't easy, but the extra hours meant extra money, and I was determined to take advantage of that. My feet ached and my mind was scrambled, often leading to strange dreams that night. Going to work without clothes on was a repetitive nightmare I had, due to the exhaustion. Very scary!

> *Staying busy makes her feel important as opposed to wasting valuable time that can otherwise make her money. She needs this time, since marriage does not spark joy. Money does.*

My first introduction to network marketing—MLMs, pyramid schemes, or whatever you want to call them— came soon after I turned twenty. It was Amway, on the night my first husband was called up to be deployed to the war.

I was way too young to understand the depths of that Amway business or how to make money at. If we hadn't been called away that day, I am sure I would have signed up, because I didn't want to upset anyone by saying "no."

Once we moved back home to Kansas, I turned twenty-one and had a baby, so I thought looking for a night job as a bartender would yield the best returns, and I was determined to keep her out of daycare. A high school friend hooked me up with an interview at a local sports bar.

When I walked in, my first thought was: *Men and TVs ... This is going to be good!* I was hired and quickly concluded I had been right. Serving beer to men while they stare at your ass equals large tips, plus I was paid more per hour when I was behind the bar. I poured a good drink, made small talk, and the dough came rolling in.

After I became pregnant for the second time, I considered finding a different career path, but my focus became paying the bills, and this job did just that. Stocking beer and maneuvering around tables was a challenge with my protruding belly, but my work ethic and desire for money prevailed. I was determined to work up to the second my water broke and then return to work shortly after giving birth.

Once I had my second daughter, I continued my night shifts at the bar, but we needed more money, so I started doing daycare for people who were working during the "normal" hours. I had no idea what that even looked like, as I hadn't ever had the desire for that type of regimented workday. When you stay home with children all day, watching *Barney*, *Sesame Street* and Disney VHS tapes, going to work in the evening seemed like a vacation. Once I got off work, that time was mine. Everyone was sleeping, so those after-work shift drinks became, let's just say, more frequent.

When my husband got into a fight at my bar, I decided it was time to find a place to work that presented itself more like a restaurant. More food, less booze. I was ready for a change after working at the sports bar for five years.

One day, I drove by a new shopping development and saw a sign in the window that caught my eye. It said "Restaurant Opening Soon," so I marched in and told them they needed to hire me as their bar manager... and they did. I had been behind the bar long enough to know that confidence isn't just about knowing your drinks; it's about showing others you know you are good at it.

Even though I would manage the bar, its focus was pub fare, and the place felt more family-orientated than drunk-centric. My income started off slow, as we were building our customer base, but when it grew, it grew very well. I started to make a ton of money, mostly in tips and mainly at night.

I worked at Pickering's Pub for twelve years, the longest stretch I ever spent at one job. I had an amazing regular crowd, and they were family. But eventually, the late-night closing shifts were getting old, just like I was, and I knew it was time for another change.

Bankers' hours didn't lure me in, and I didn't have any experience other than the service industry, but I was good at reading people like a book and still am. Well, except for hubby number two—he was a challenge. After researching possible career paths, I chose real estate. The main thing that attracted me was the flexibility to show houses when my schedule allowed. I went to school and obtained my license.

With my personality, I used emotions to make decisions and ignored some of the hard, true facts, like that it takes years to get established as an agent, and you must spend money to do mailings and flyers before making a dime. Waiting for the money to start rolling in from my new career wasn't an option for me, so I continued to work part-time at the bar to make ends meet.

Little fun fact: my email address was real8gent@aol.com. First, that seriously makes me feel old, as I used AOL mail (one of the first email servers known to man). Second, now you can see my corny humor.

I still have that black-and-white business card, my first of many. My entrepreneurial spirit started to form at this time. Often, I saw opportunities when others only saw challenges. I craved new obstacles and was fueled by money.

Working as an agent part-time didn't work well, however, and divorce number one had begun, so I shifted my attention back to bartending full time and quit real estate. That is what paid the bills.

> "If you follow the money, you'll lose your dreams.
> If you follow your dreams, the money will come."
> —George Collopy

Dreams of Change

After having my daughters, I was intrigued by the whole birthing process. Not that mine was perfect or even enjoyable, but the nurses were like heroes to me, and I wanted to be that for others. This desire bloomed into dreams of becoming a labor and delivery nurse. Despite their rotating shifts, it was better than working nights, and they made good money—which my dreams always needed.

I began taking classes at the local community college to become a nurse someday and finally do something for myself. To get my feet wet in this line of work, I started working at a hospital as a nurse assistant after I passed my CNA certification. I was assigned to the fourth floor, covering post-heart transplants, GI patients, and random geriatric issues. *Not* mothers and babies.

Some days were really shitty, *literally*: changing soiled bedding while the patient lay in it proved to be a challenging task. I should have been changing baby diapers, I thought, not adults. The shifts were twelve hours long and physically draining, but I found joy in some parts of the job. Conversing with the elderly, even if they were battling dementia, became one of the highlights of my day. Since I was so close to my grandmother, I couldn't imagine treating them any way other than with love and compassion.

I worked on completing the prerequisites I needed before applying to nursing school. Anatomy and physiology classes were daunting, and the school work proved to be too much for me to juggle while being a working single mom.

> *Yet again, she comes to realize what being a single mom demands. The hospital job income is nothing compared to what she can make at the bars. She feels like a failure again. Life seems different now, and her dreams will have to take a back seat. The Money Monster is in control, as it has to be, to pay the bills.*

Once again, I found myself back at the bar, working full time. It felt like being stuck in a never-ending cycle. Every time I tried to work somewhere else, I was pulled back to the same place. The bar had become my fallback, my constant, but also a reminder that things weren't going the way I had hoped.

When I got married the second time, hubby number two moved in with us, since I'd received the house as part of the asset division with hubby one. His job title was *golf pro*, not to be confused with a pro golfer, who earns a hefty paycheck!

I didn't know how much money he had or what his paycheck looked like, but I wasn't too worried about it, as I did all right without his contributions. The gifts and romantic getaways he treated me to made me assume he was financially secure. You know what the word *ass-u-me* can do for you, right? Eye roll.

Thinking we needed a fresh start in a house my ex hadn't lived in, Hubby Two expressed the desire to move, to which I reluctantly agreed. With the newfound knowledge I'd acquired in real estate school, I decided to sell this home, "For Sale By Owner." The beautiful remodel job I had done, with fruit wallpaper borders and café curtains to match, would surely get top dollar. (Don't laugh—it was the "in" thing, I promise.)

There was good equity in this house, but we needed money up front to start the construction of our new dream home. My parents came to the rescue and lent us the down payment, until we got our old house sold. I listed it, and, in under twenty-four hours, it sold with no inspections and for full price!

This was such an exciting time for us. Making a house feel like a home was something I enjoyed, and I couldn't wait to get my hands on this new project.

We selected a lot that would fit a California split, four-bedroom home on a cul-de-sac in a neighborhood I had dreamed of living in someday. Growing up, this is where my rich friends lived. The homes in the area were newer, with pools and an elementary school right nearby. Since I grew up in an income-guided community, I wanted my girls to have this nice area to grow up in, now that I could afford it.

I picked out all the colors, fixtures, and flooring. This house would be Art Deco style, with lots of silver, straight lines, and primary colors. Plus, a purple-felted pool table in the front living room, by the fireplace. Money was no object as I made my selections.

> *Proudly, she has earned good money from her efforts at buying, remodeling, and selling her home, which gives her confidence. Even her parents are excited for the new place, as it is closer to where they live. Their approval is what she yearns for. At thirty years old, she believes this next decade will be all about her!*

Since I sold *my* house so quickly and our new one would take six months to build, we needed a temporary place to live. Hubby Two knew a golf member who would let us live in one of his rentals for free. *Free*—one of my favorite four-letter F words!

This old farmhouse didn't even have an oven, only a stovetop and a microwave for cooking, but we had to make it work. It was our only option, after all, and it was temporary. Since it was located in the next town over, outside of my girls' school district, I had to drive them thirty minutes each way to school every day.

Our new house would need lots of cool furnishings, so I found another job waitressing at lunch time at a local bar and grill. This allowed me to continue bartending at night and still shuttle the girls around town. Working never bothered me, and having two jobs seemed like the answer—for now. There were times I wondered if it was worth it. The stress of multiple jobs while driving all over town was exhausting. It seemed, as soon as one task was finished, another one was waiting. This house was the motivation I needed to keep on truckin'!

> *Her hard work ethic and love for being in charge has kept many relationships afloat, financially. She has to prove her worth in their relationship, and that is when the Money Monster loves to get inside her mind. If she makes more money, she will be worthy of her desires.*

The Cash Crash

Not long after we moved in, things suddenly shifted. Hubby Two decided he didn't like the golfing gig anymore, so he went to work for one of the golf members who owned a liquor store, the same guy who let us live in his house while we built ours. His new career was in outside sales, growing the restaurant and bar wholesale business, which allowed him lots of free time. I began to resent him for that, as I was working my ass off to make ends meet. Again, stuck in a never-ending grind, always being the one to hustle. The feeling of being undervalued while giving my all was suffocating me.

My credit was great, therefore we financed a lot of stuff for our new home, but I knew the interest on these purchases would compile quickly, if we didn't get them paid off. Real estate had taught me the value of a good credit score and its importance for obtaining not only homes but anything else you desire.

I even bought myself a bright-yellow Mustang to sit in the new driveway. It was gorgeous. (The car, not the driveway!) Being around hubby number one had grown my love for hot rods and the need for speed. The kids' friends thought I was so hip when I picked them up from school—I will not deny, I *did* feel pretty cool. My girls, not so much.

Maybe it was my Mustang midlife crisis. Life seemed to be going well.

> *If she only knew about the real crisis heading her way. The new house and furnishings are a symbol of achievement... Or are they just filling a void from her past life? There are rumors about his past that she ignores. Her voice is quieted by the yearning for this new life, filled with lots of material things. But the questions around who he has been start to emerge.*

He spent less time working and more time, well, I'm not sure. One thing I did know: he wasn't getting his sales bonuses, so his contributions to the household income slowly declined.

The bills started piling up, and before I knew it, we couldn't pay them. No one could find out. There's something incredibly heavy about being unable to pay bills. It's not just about the money—it's the weight of feeling like you're falling behind, unable to keep up. You try to balance everything, including the checkbook, while juggling all your other priorities. But then, life hits you with an unexpected setback—*HIM*!

The next slap across the face (not physically) was finding out he'd been fired months ago. Not only was he unemployed, but he hung out constantly at a casino or bar while spending what little money we did have. The only solution I could come up with was to make more money, so I found myself working multiple jobs once again.

We were now waist-high in debt with no hope of getting out. That son of a bitch! While I tried to figure out a plan, there were more signs that it was time to get out.

FINDING HER

I am pretty sure he was cheating and using drugs, but I couldn't prove it nor did I really care anymore. The embarrassing letters, bill collectors' calls, and notices on the door were wearing me down.

> *How can she let this happen to her and the girls, again? When she threatens to leave, he promises to get a job, but those empty words fuel the hatred building inside. It seems like the right time for her to get out. She doesn't want to stay in this house, as it's become a constant reminder of the unpaid bills, but where will she go? This Monster merges with the Money Monster to give her another blow.*

Since I was the one forking out all the money to pay the bills that *could* be paid, like the mortgage, I assumed the girls and I would be staying there, in the house. I thought of ways to escape the nightmare, while stashing away some of the cash. I needed a fast solution to this financial shit show we were in.

As I planned my next move, Hubby Two sternly announced that he would not leave our house. I'd had no idea he was so manipulative until now, and I grew scared at the thought of what living with him could look like for me and my girls. He had been lying about paying some bills, and the mortgage payment was one of them.

As the bank started to threaten foreclosure, I knew the damage had already been done to my credit score, so my focus became how to get the hell out of there. My emotions were so mixed at this point. I felt heartbroken, betrayed, and frustrated as hell. But it was time for mama bear to protect her cubs.

One day, while he was out of the house, doing God knows what, the girls and I packed a few bags and left. The bank would lock the doors and sell our belongings soon, and I didn't want the girls to be there to witness that disheartening takeover.

Then I wondered, how could I rent anything with credit that had crashed in a matter of months? Living at my parents' home at the age of thirty-two wasn't a long-term option, but I decided I could force myself to go there for a few weeks during my search. Since I wasn't used to reporting in or being judged for what I did, those weeks felt like a lifetime. I was grateful but also annoyed.

After applying for rentals and being denied time after time, I turned to friends for advice. I felt depressed and embarrassed, like I had failed at my personal and financial life. And there was no way I would ask my parents for help: I had made this bed and had to lie in it.

A friend of mine whom I had met while bartending generously offered to cosign for me. At the time, he was dating a girl who lived in a nice area with some duplexes available for rent. I don't think he ever told his girlfriend that he'd cosigned for my lease, and it became our little secret.

Guess who that guy ended up being…? My current husband, Mark! His signature gave me the boost I needed to begin this battle. Maybe he had an alternative motive? I didn't care, as it was the only lifeline I had to grab.

We moved into the three-bedroom, two-bath duplex with a fenced-in backyard that was the perfect place for my girls and me to start over, once again. The asshole, Hubby Two, wouldn't let us back into the house to get anything other than the girls' bedroom furniture, so we made do with garage sale items and a thirteen-inch TV.

All the "stuff" we had purchased for that "dream home" meant nothing to me at this point. Although I felt overwhelmed by the control that he still had over my me, it was time to reclaim my life.

My parents wanted him out of my life just as much as I did, so they gave me the money to start divorce proceedings. One weekend, when he left to go out of town, my friends and I conjured up a plan to retrieve some of my valuables from the house where he still lived, for free!

The house happened to be in both of our names, so I was able to call a locksmith and have the locks changed. I had heard from a few mutual friends that he had sold many of the bigger items already, so those that remained were my target. Get him where it hurts!

We loaded things up and took them to a location where he couldn't find them. I worried, if I took them to my house, he would come looking for them. I didn't need that drama. When he returned to find the locks changed and items gone, his serious threats scared me into returning everything we'd taken.

If I detached myself from what we had together, he couldn't touch it. That became my new plan.

> *She takes everything back, scared for the last time. She is done being controlled by him and the money. Her sanity is worth more than stuff. Hopefully, she will hear her, now that outside interference has cleared.*

That jerk lived in that house, payment free, for a year before the bank finally took it over and kicked him out. I lost so much—not just money, but my pride. The community I had once dreamed of being a part of, growing up, had become a battleground I never wanted to see again.

As if I hadn't lost enough, my lack of money caused me to do the unimaginable. I called Ford Motor Credit and told them to come repossess my Mustang. The payment and insurance were too much, and I couldn't bear another creditor going unpaid. While the neighbors peered out their windows and watched my car being towed away, more of my dreams faded into the distance, along with my once-excellent credit.

Sadly, the next attorney I had to hire was a bankruptcy lawyer. After it was filed, the collection calls ceased, and I was able to make small payments to the lawyer for his services.

> *She has to swallow her pride and focus on taking care of the girls. She feels so guilty about turning her back on all that debt, since she wasn't raised to be lazy or a burden on others. It becomes time to distance herself from the old and welcome the process of discovering the new.*

Once the bankruptcy was done, the divorce would be soon, too. I erased #2 (perfect number for that shithead) from all parts of my life, and when I appeared in court for the final proceedings, I asked the judge for a name change.

The judge granted my wishes, so I took my mother's maiden name. Angela Anderson would be the new me. I was proud to have that family name!

"What you can and can't afford is all in your mind."
—Jen Sincero, *You Are a Badass at Making Money: Master the Mindset of Wealth*

Dil-Dough

When I became single, *finally just me*, I was the one in control. That empowered me to find additional ways to make more money, the one thing I was a seasoned pro at now.

When opportunity knocks, sometimes it comes at strange doorways. My next opportunity came in the form of sex toys.

I attended a girl's night out at a friend's house, a Passion Night Party. I am sure some of you have been to these home parties, where they sell lotions, potions, toys, and lingerie. The party turned out to be really fun, and the host who presented the party had stocked enough inventory so we could go home with our purchases and not have to wait weeks for things to be shipped, unlike most home parties I had attended before.

While we were making our purchases privately, my friend asked if I would host a party or consider becoming a consultant. Once she explained the commission structure, I was easily convinced that this would be my next venture.

This became my first network-marketing gig. Booking parties came easy to me, though who doesn't love a good girl's night? Plus, my guests' husbands could care less how much they spent on these novelties, so the wallets opened easily, and the ladies spent away. Some nights, I would make $500 while I drank wine and enjoyed some girl time. This cash cow was perfect for me, without requiring much effort.

Even though I did pretty well with bartending and selling dildos, after a few years, I knew I needed to find a "real" job in the near future. The late nights at the bar and holding these parties began to wear on me, especially when I had a couples' party. The men were intrigued and asked so many questions. One guy even had the balls to ask where the G-spot was. I was embarrassed for him. At times, these would last hours longer than just the girls' night, and ironically, I wouldn't sell as much; it seemed the women were not as comfortable with their purchases at a co-ed event. The men just changed the environment. It was time to move on from that battery-operated gig.

One of my neighbors told me about an opportunity to work for a copier company. This would be a corporate job, which was something I really didn't want, but I felt it was time to grow up and get out into the real work force.

My friend thought I would be great at this, due to my personality and customer-service skills. Thankfully, I was offered a job, and that allowed me to quit my late-night shifts selling alcohol and vibrators.

This eight-to-five job had small pay plus a big commission structure; this wasn't foreign to me, since I had worked for hourly plus tips for all my life. It didn't take me long to realize this was not a women's world—the men clearly dominated the industry, unlike my prior food-service jobs.

Cold calling included tons of rejection, and I often didn't meet my quota. I had spent my whole life waiting on customers who *wanted* what I had to sell; this was the complete opposite case. I knocked on countless doors before finding a company willing to spend money on a machine that upgraded how fast their copies were made.

The gatekeepers (receptionists), as we called them, were seasoned hard-asses who couldn't wait for people like us to walk in the door, so they could tell us, "Sorry, not interested." Simply getting an appointment with a decision-maker proved to be the biggest hurdle, and I did not seem to have the personality to get over the objections.

I quickly grew tired of this job's negative vibe. The cocky assholes I worked with thought they were God's gift to making copies and were on my last nerve. It's not like I disliked authority or wasn't a hard worker. The problem was more the lack of being able to have fun and express my creative side. It seemed like time to find something else, again.

I typically spent most of the days out in my territory, making sales calls. However, on this one particular day, I just happened to be at my desk, doing paperwork. A headhunter mistakenly called my sales line. It seems I was at the right place at the right time.

After we both discovered he had reached the wrong person, he decided to go ahead and explain that he represented a furniture rental company that had been looking for an outside sales rep. This sounded right up my alley, since I loved furniture and had been gaining skills in sales, so I sent in my résumé and landed an interview.

During the questioning, I was asked why I would be a good candidate, and my immediate response was, "Furniture is sexier than copiers." I can't believe I said that!

I was simply telling the truth, which I guess was what got me hired. Or was it because I happened to be interviewed by two men? Who knows! This was a salaried position with great benefits. The sales calls were friendly, and I loved my new job.

Mark and I were married the following year. Yippee! After a few months, we put all our funds together and decided he would handle the finances in our relationship.

Obviously, my track record with money wasn't the strongest, and I happily handed over that responsibility to him. Together, we made good money, and finally, the bankruptcy felt like a thing of the past.

Over a few years, my job was restructured time and time again, when new management cycled in and out. Due to one reorganization in our company, I was forced to work inside and do retail sales. This required me to be in the showroom, working later in the evening and on the weekends. As a mom, this was not the ideal situation for me.

The constantly changing roles within the company and the corporate bullshit from the top made everyone cranky and the work environment suck. I began to daydream about doing something different, but the consistent paycheck and benefits kept me there, for now.

> *He wants her to be happy, so he spoils her with gifts, trips, and anything she wants. She has endured so much and deserves everything—even if it puts them in debt. The house they live in becomes a money pit, and finances start to look scary again. The Money Monster begins to rear its ugly head once again.*

Having only one job left me feeling like I was not enough. That's when other network marketing opportunities popped in and out of my life: Mary Kay, Tastefully Simple, and Silpada. I dabbled in many over the years but never found the right fit.

I liked the concept and freedom, but the home parties had become harder to book, since most women in my circle of friends felt burnt out after attending so many. If they did attend, they didn't spend like they had, during my last MLM. The pressure behind it made me feel gross inside, like

I was a greasy salesman, something I knew plenty about from my copier-sales days.

Coffee Currency

One of my co-workers, who is still a dear friend of mine, mentioned that an acquaintance of hers had investigated a new coffee franchise that had expanded into our area. I didn't drink coffee and knew nothing about making it, but this idea intrigued me.

One of my many entrepreneurial daydreams involved a restaurant. I missed that environment, but I also knew it was not the best fit for a family. I had witnessed so many relationships be destroyed by the influences of alcohol. The hospitality industry happened to be known for that, so I shoved the restaurant idea out the window. But coffee, I could handle.

I began researching what it took to form an LLC and what opportunities were out there for business loans. Researching is something I love to do, so this part of the journey turned into the best part. Would you believe there are bikini coffee shops out there? The idea of serving up coffee in a swimsuit was not an idea I wanted to entertain. Imagine spilling hot coffee on your boob…? No, thanks! In the past, I had heard boys tell me my tits were *hot* but not in this context.

I wasn't too keen on the idea of a franchise at first, but after spending many hours investigating and contemplating all the pros and cons, I concluded this direction was my best bet for success. I contacted the developer and started to drive around town, scouting for my future location.

During this process, I became aware of an existing coffee shop that was up for sale. It was a walk-in only, with no drive thru, on the corner of a very busy intersection. From all the knowledge I had gained doing my diligent research, I knew that the number of cars driving by every day was a huge key to having a successful business. The owner of this space was moving soon, so it seemed like a dream come true.

Mark and I figured out a way to come up with the money for all the initial fees associated with buying a franchise, and I obtained a loan for the rest of the expenses. The existing business was established and growing, so that income would take care of the monthly payment, lease, and other costs. With the owners leaving town soon, I had two weeks to learn the business and how to make all the fancy coffee concoctions. Thankfully, I inherited two seasoned baristas to keep things running smoothly, while I learned the ropes.

Serving a cup of coffee with a smile was in my wheelhouse, and I rocked it! I knew all the customers' names and what they drank, just like back in the old bartending days, but with people who were sober and happy versus drunk and angry. The bonus was we closed each night at 8:00 p.m., not 2:00 a.m.!

I didn't give myself a salary, as most small businesses can't afford that at the beginning, but I did pay myself an hourly wage plus tips—we know I love those cash tips. In a roundabout way, I had bought myself a job but also a fulfillment of belonging and the satisfaction of success… I loved it!

I had served poison in the toxic environment of a bar for years, but now, being able to make others smile without intoxicating them felt like a moment of redemption.

> *The coffee shop becomes her identity, and she is proud of what she has. She does something most wouldn't, which makes her feel exponentially like a badass. Her self-esteem rises, but little does she know, there are a few untamed things brewing. She has to learn some lessons more than once.*

"Hard work keeps the wrinkles out of the mind and spirit
—Helena Rubinstein

Barista Break

Meanwhile, back on the home front, Mark and I were witnessing the collapse of the economy, which led us to diving into ours. We had been vicariously enjoying vacations, new chrome for our motorcycles, and putting a shit-ton into our house, which sadly had turned into a money pit.

We sat down and wrote out all our expenses and income. This gave us a shocking perspective—let's just say we were in the red. And not just that. As we read the latest statements, we noticed that our creditors had raised our interest rates with no warning. Not just a little, but over eighteen percent%! We had been paying very little or none, prior to that.

This was in late 2008, and we had more credit card debt than either of us cared to admit. The kicker was: the banks weren't lending any money. This had been triggered by an increase in high-risk mortgages and defaults on those debts, which, in turn, had led to a major collapse of financial institutions. While we were confident in our credit score, we figured we may as well try to get a consolidation loan or explore our options to decrease some of this interest that was eating up our finances.

We called Bank of America, where we banked and had done business for years. As we inquired about the astronomical interest rates, they shut down our credit and closed our accounts. No kidding—while we were on the phone with them!

> *She feels ashamed she let her debt get this high but, at the same time, is proud she has her credit back on track. The Monster returns, and this time, it is created by others who are in a situation like the one she found herself in, years ago. She will have to use her prior battle to ignite this new one.*

We were stuck paying huge interest rates with no recourse. It was time to dig in, as I was not losing this battle! Mark and I hammered away at the budget, fine-tuning every detail. We sold what we didn't need and did what we could to get our money pit on the market. It took us three years to finally sell that house; meanwhile, we made some progress on debt.

Thankfully, mortgage rates settled down, and after that house, we decided there would be no more 1970s homes for us. That one had been riddled with constant projects.

We built a beautiful home on a gorgeous lot not far from where we had lived. As the economy grew, so did the equity in our new home. When we watched a few homes in our neighborhood go on the market, we realized just how much we had. This was the break we needed.

The next day, I listed our home on Zillow, For Sale by Owner. It sold in twenty-four hours, and we decided to live in an apartment until we figured out our next move. This turned out to be a smart decision and allowed us to pay off *all* that debt. We vowed to *never* be in debt again.

Back to the Grind

I joined the local Chamber of Commerce and worked to make my coffee shop one of the best places in town to meet up and chat with a friend or business client. These networking events allowed me to connect with so many potential customers. At the same time, though, this roped me back into network marketing, as many were there to build their teams.

I met the Twins (more on them in another chapter), and they recruited me as a coach with Beachbody. This was an MLM that sold shakes, at-home workout DVDs, and other supplements. Of course, owning a coffee shop wasn't enough for me. It was a nice side gig to support women in their weight-loss journey. Running online Facebook groups helped me stay accountable for my workouts, too.

Even though I had successfully grown my sales numbers, eventually I had to come to the realization that, with limited parking spots and no drive-thru, the coffee shop had reached its full potential and couldn't bring in much more monthly income. Between machines needing repairs and the franchise requiring us to change our computer system, the QuickBooks was showing we were in the red, and I got nervous. There were times when I had to pay the monthly sales tax that we owed to the state a little late. So, my new task became moving money around. I found myself at a crossroads again and began the search for something else to make ends meet.

The urge to learn more about health and fitness led me to a book called *Buddha Belly*. As I read the book, I was intrigued for several reasons. First, I had a very similar story, and second, the author taught gut-health coach certification.

While I juggled the budget, the employees, and my Beachbody groups, I began the online courses with the Holistic Wellness Coaching Academy. As I learned about the gut, my health started to take a turn for the worse, and the energy I'd once had diminished. (Details of this are coming up in the last chapter.)

By this point, I'd lost my two key employees and had a hard time finding any help. I worked more hours with less joy while feeling like shit. Mark was approaching retirement, and we were looking to buy a lake cabin, so selling the coffee shop seemed like the smartest thing to do for ourselves, financially.

> *The feeling of being a badass deteriorates, just as her health does. She will have no job to attach her identity to, which she has always relied on. At the same time, the Gut Monster begins to emerge as this transpires.*

I sold the coffee shop and bought our little cabin on Lake of the Ozarks with the proceeds. After owning the store for eight years, the satisfaction of giving someone a morning smile is still one of the things I miss the most. But as they say, everything happens for a reason. I truly believe this.

When Covid came, the new owners had to shut down the business, and the landlord ended up bulldozing the building to put in a huge gas station. Thank you, Universe!

Holistic Dime Bags

While my health kept me at home much of the time, I began exploring new ways to earn an income. I had quit Beachbody coaching and came across a new MLM that offered natural supplements, including CBD oil. This new product line made dollar signs pop into my "Little Orphan Angie" eyes. Something I could pursue from home while searching for answers to my declining health.

When I started using the CBD oil, I noticed a real improvement in my health. That experience lit a fire in me— I realized, by sharing my story, I could not only earn an income but also could help others who were struggling like I was.

Even though I did well promoting the CBD, after a while I grew weary of the business model. Selling came easy, but recruiting was not my strong suit, and if I wanted to work my way up the ladder, I needed to work on building a larger team. That felt like having employees again.

The Holistic Gut Health Coaching course I had been taking online was on hold while I focused on *my* gut. Sadly, I ended up having surgery and didn't finish that course in the allotted time, due to my health.

The previous fall we had upgraded our place on the lake from our small weekend cabin to a larger home that was more suitable for full-time living. A month after my surgery, Mark retired, and we moved to the lake.

One day, while scrolling social media, I felt a nudge from the Universe. The founder of the Gut Coaching Academy appeared on my Instagram. Honestly, I had long forgotten about that school and hadn't seen any posts from her for months. Those dreams of being a coach had vanished when my bad health appeared. After she'd showed up on my news feed multiple times, I decided to take a leap of faith and message her to ask if it would be possible to pick up where I had left off.

Understanding the health issues that caused me to drop out, she agreed to make an exception and allow me to return and continue the program. I am not one to keep a lot of things, but for some reason, I had kept all my books and notes from a few years prior. So, back to school I went!

At the same time, Missouri legalized medicinal marijuana, and after my positive experience with CBD, I grew more curious about the cannabis industry. The Cannabis Coaching Institute also popped up on my radar. Another nudge? So, I enrolled in that program simultaneously. Why not add more to my plate, right? Managing multiple things at once has always energized me, though this time, I might have pushed myself a bit too far.

In fact, I also enrolled in a "Better Way Business" program with another author whose book I had been reading. Her faith-based book had me sitting quietly asking for answers to questions about what I should do next. *Quiet* wasn't a word my personality aligned with, but it was worth a shot. So, I started to get in tune with what my purpose would be. I soaked in the bathtub, asked for guidance from above, and then silenced my mind to receive whatever came to me.

That's when the name *Gut Girl Coaching* came to me. This was the first time I recognized this voice in my head. Before, most thoughts and ideas I heard were all over the place, but this one was clear and concise. I immediately got out of the bath, wrapped myself up in a towel, and bought the domain GutGirlCoaching.com. This answer was exactly what I'd been looking for.

After I graduated from all of the courses, I started coaching with a holistic whole-body solution to better health and general well-being as key aspects of my business. I assisted clients with weight loss and created personalized eight-week plans. I helped them to improve sleep and address restless leg syndrome, gut issues, and a variety of other health issues. Cannabis was one option some of my clients explored.

This is when I realized I had turned into a true entrepreneur and would never work for anyone else again. Armed with knowledge I had learned in cannabis school, I started to make my own line of CBD and CBG called Flower Power. Since I wasn't interested in just selling oil, coaching became my main focus, but it was nice to have this additional weapon in my toolbox. I still provide it to past clients and friends. The ability to make my own medicine is empowering!

> *She can see some progress in the battle with the Money Monster by finding her true purpose. The monetary goals she's focused on in her jobs become a thing of the past, as she truly listens to her, more and more. At times, her nudges are misinterpreted, but she grows excited, knowing she finally is on the right path.*

Of course, not all ideas are successful ideas. Owning the coffee shop had not only turned me into a coffee snob, it also turned me into the girl with the funny coffee mugs. Throughout the years, I collected mugs with silly sayings. Many of them gifted to me by friends and family. I used them for social media posts and had over fifty of them at one point. Since I was familiar with developing a website from my coaching business, I decided to hire a graphic designer and then opened an online coffee mug store. Online retail proved to be a different animal, though, and with Amazon as competition, it was a flop! I learned that my inspirational mugs were best used for uplighting those on social media, rather than for making a few bucks. Live and learn, I suppose.

As I coached clients, I became aware of some roadblocks I was having around money. With all of my certifications, I was worth more than I charged, but I struggled with charging more for my services. I enrolled in a mindset course to dig deeper into what was holding me back. During that course, I discovered that the feeling of *unworthiness* played a huge role in my life. Especially when it came to money.

The mantra "I am worthy" became a powerful tool in my personal battle. It wasn't just a phrase—it was a reminder that I had the strength to face the challenges and overcome mental roadblocks. I strategically placed Post-it Notes around my home, to keep this idea at the forefront of my mind and to keep me grounded during tough times.

I was presented with an opportunity to partner with a medical marijuana doctor. This hippie doctor (yes, long hair and a member of a very popular band, back in the day) had retired, but he'd pivoted when medical marijuana became legal in Missouri. Under that new law, doctors could prescribe medical cards based on records, but they were not trained on what types of cannabis work for what ailments.

What a great partnership that became. This doctor referred patients to me, and I started to make a difference in peoples' lives, which made me feel proud. There were times when I would meet clients at the dispensary and guide them on their purchases. Walking into a dispensary and choosing the right product can be scary, especially for the elderly, who were my favorite clients to assist.

Sadly, two years later, that all changed when the state approved recreational marijuana use. Since you didn't need a doctor's card anymore, the leads dried up. At about the same time, social media started to become a negative space for me, with the mental anguish outweighing the outcome.

Mark and I had been discussing traveling more, so I decided to retire from my coaching business. I closed the website down and cleared out my client files. There was a mix of relief and sadness. Even though I knew it was the right decision, there was still a sense of loss, as a chapter of my life had ended. I would guess most people who retire feel this way, too.

Property Payoffs

After I retired and all of our home remodeling projects were completed, Mark and I decided to spend our winters somewhere warm. We had grown tired of the cold Missouri winters and were bored with our annual trips to Mexico. Texas and Florida were states we considered, but the humidity there sent us searching for somewhere drier.

We decided that Arizona would become our new escape away from the cold winters. Some of our friends had moved there recently, which made it even more appealing than the other locations. The next task was looking for the right community.

It was important for us to find one that had many activities, as well as the right vibe. After touring a couple of places that allowed children, we came to the conclusion that an over-55 community would be the best fit. We wanted more of a resort feel, with swimming pools and pickleball as two of our top "must haves."

I wasn't fifty-five yet, but thankfully, Mark would qualify. I now joke that I married him years ago so I could get into one of these resorts! As we pulled into the Sundance RV Resort in Casa Grande, Arizona, we knew we had found our new winter getaway.

The entrance had enormous metal sculptures of horses, and the streets were lined with palm trees. Everyone we saw waved and said hello. The property was very clean, and the list of activities was like being on a cruise ship. Something was going on every day, all day!

We found an adorable park model home in the community and decided to make the purchase. (In case you didn't know—I did not—a park model is a tiny home permanently set up with electricity and water.)

At this point, we had quit drinking, and the appeal of living on the lake was dwindling. Lake homes were selling like hotcakes, and we had new visions for our life ahead. Although we made many great memories with our families and friends while living there, the reality was it required a lot of work that would restrict our future plans to travel more.

My knowledge of real estate and our love for remodeling allowed us to turn a good profit each time we sold a house. (Well except for our first one—that was a money pit.) The money we made from one enabled us to level up with each move. The lake house would be the icing on the cake: selling it would put us in a position to pay cash for the new home we were building back in the city.

> *She never saw this coming. Blinded by the Money Monster, she can't see all she's accomplished through her hard work. Her vision becomes clearer every day. Money is not her focus now. Her purpose is.*

From Pennies to Penmanship

After moving from the lake, I found myself with plenty of extra time on my hands. I was inspired by a thirty-day journaling challenge to begin writing every morning. I loved what flowed from my pen onto paper, which ignited my desire to write a book. I bought a spiral-bound notebook and started writing about my journey with Crohn's disease. That was in October 2022.

I knew from speaking on stage at past CBD conventions that people were interested in hearing my story. They often approached me afterward and thanked me for sharing, explaining that they themselves were struggling or knew someone who had similar battles. This fueled my passion to share my health journey, but I never knew how to bring that to fruition. The writing started to feel meaningless, so I stuffed my notebook into a drawer.

> *She is writing a chronological story of her life, but the focus is her Gut Monster. The Mirror Monster has limiting beliefs, telling*

her she is not a good writer and will never be an author. She writes for six months and then stops.

I always looked forward to my monthly meetings with my cannabis school connections. Even though I had hung up my coaching hat, I enjoyed hearing about what projects others were working on or what they were struggling with in the industry.

One call featured a few teachers and students who were beginning a project to publish a book, with each chapter featuring people who had been positively affected by cannabis. As you will learn later, I certainly had been! Others on the call were messaging me privately via the chat, urging me to share my story. I was the first to sign up for the "Dare to Share" project; ecstatic to know my story may finally be heard. This was another nudge I could not ignore.

As the months passed by, the coordinators were having a difficult time recruiting enough people to be part of the project. The project kept being pushed back, which frustrated me to no end. Although I had picked up the pen again, the delays were making me weary.

Two months later, I received an email that gave me a shiver down my spine—not from being cold, but something deeper. It was as if the Universe was sending me back onto the right path.

The project developers for the "Dare to Share" project decided, if they had a completed chapter to present to prospects, it would spark more interest. They wanted me to be a beta writer! This opportunity involved one-on-one coaching from a former cannabis classmate who happened to be an English teacher. In the past, I considered hiring a ghostwriter or a book coach, but the expense kept me away. I was afraid I'd fail *and* waste money.

Under this plan, my coach and I would meet a few times a month and work together on new writing prompts, to help start forming my story. But just as my hopes grew, another roadblock derailed my writing efforts. The whole project was called off, and my words would not be seen. I closed my notebook and put down my pen, once again.

> *She thinks she has been in tune with what the Universe has in store for her. Could this be another sign to stop writing? Why is this happening to her again? She lets life go on, and the desire to tell her story fades just as the other dreams have.*

As another year passed, a new sign appeared. A girl I had followed for years on social media suddenly reappeared in my feed. She had taken a break from posting on social media, just as I had. She and I had similar gut issues, and even though she didn't know me, I had grown to know her through her posts and the struggles she had endured.

As her posts began to pop up more often on my feed, she shared the exciting news that she was writing a book! A few months after it was published, I purchased a copy. I was eager to dive in but decided to wait until our upcoming RV trip, thinking it would be the perfect time to start. I wanted to be in a place where I could take it all in.

I was hooked from the first page, and there were many stories in her book that paralleled experiences in my life. Each morning, after I took my hikes, I lay in the sun and read. Little did I know, this would eventually inspire me to pick up the pen again.

While on our RV trip, I tried really hard to steer clear of social media and just be in the moment. When we returned home, I began to see her posts again and noticed she offered horse-riding retreats. This was something we did *not* have in common. Don't get me wrong, I like horses, but I am more attracted to retreats geared toward hiking or yoga.

Then one day, a different offering from her popped up in my feed. She was hosting a two-day writing course. I got chills (hello, Universe) when I saw this and signed up immediately. Some of the material covered in the workshop was similar to what I had learned previously from my prior book project. However, the new insights gave me a fresh perspective, reigniting my excitement about writing.

On the final day, she explained the process she had followed to publish her book and talked about the people she'd collaborated with. My ears perked up, and my curiosity was instantly sparked. I asked for more details, and she emailed me the next day.

The following Saturday, I attended a three-hour meditation retreat. Ironically, the instructor provided us all writing journals and pens to use. Another sign, oh my! That day, I had a powerful vision during meditation—one that truly changed me. I'll share that revelation with you soon.

> *The Universe screams now, and all she can do is listen. She knows this will be the next step to sharing her words. The stars align, and it proves to be the time. She isn't going to let anyone or anything get in her way—not even the Money Monster!*

After receiving the information about the publisher, I filled out a request for an appointment, and the following

Friday, I spent an hour on a Zoom call with Landon Hail Press. I explained my idea for a book, and the editor-in-chief went into details about their process. After the call, if I was interested in proceeding, the next step was to submit a sample of my writing.

I provided them with a writing sample and then had to wait while her team reviewed what I had turned in. I began journaling, meditating and reading a book about writing as a way of passing the time, while simultaneously telling the Universe I was ready!

Two weeks later, the email came... I had an offer! To be honest, that was a day to be remembered—a true turning point in my healing journey. I am now doing something I could never have imagined, one that feels perfectly aligned with who I am and what I am meant to do: write this book!

> *While writing, she concludes that the job she feels afraid of most is herself. Her words will now be seen, and this will deliver the final blow to the Money Monster, as she has found her place in the world.*

To those who are starting out in life, please take some free advice from me. Stay away from credit cards or financing when you need to buy anything, unless it is interest free. Purchase furniture and decor from thrift stores and Facebook marketplace—there are so many resources for this now. If an item doesn't spark joy, then sell it.

I have learned that minimalist living can bring more happiness than all the "stuff." Use the beauty of our world as entertainment—it is free! No restaurant food, car, furniture, handbag, or set of nails can make you feel better than being debt-free.

ANGIE LICKLITER

You are rich, my friend… More than you know.

"Be happy with what you have,
while working for what you want."
–Helen Keller

Monster 3

Food

ONCE I BEGAN TO TRULY reflect on the things that had been controlling my life, I saw how they weren't just holding me back—they were slowly eating away at me. The Mirror Monster had persuaded me to believe that food was the answer to all my problems. Conniving creatures they are!

The Dreaded Dinner

My first food memories aren't comforting. They're filled with tension. I remember being forced to eat vegetables and other so-called "healthy" foods on my plate. There was no choice or conversation around what we ate, no matter how much I hated what was on it. There were many nights when I sat at the table for an hour, trying to chew that last bite without any moisture left in my mouth. Even if it was a tough piece of meat, we were not allowed to drink milk to wash down a bite.

I tried to prove a point, and I guess my parents were doing the same. In my mind, those meals were just another way for my dad to control us. But now, I do agree with the concept of encouraging kids to try at least one bite, since they typically refuse new foods without tasting them.

My brother and I would wait for our parents to turn around and then spit out the chewed food into our napkins and quickly drink some milk. These tactics didn't work for very long, though, before we were busted. Then, it was off to the corner for a five-minute, nose-to-the-wall punishment. The odor of the lead paint filled my nose as I breathed heavily. What the hell does putting my nose in the corner for five minutes have to do with spitting out a tough piece of meat into my napkin? Cook better, people!

Like my grandmother, my mom made sure there were plenty of homemade treats in the house. The cookies she made with the Frosted Flakes were called Tiger Cookies, and they were my favorite. The contrast between the crunch and the gooey chocolate was irresistible.

Once while working on a school project, I noticed that my Elmer's glue bottle had crusted on the top, clogging the tip. For some stupid reason, I thought it was a good idea to go show my mom, who was in the kitchen, mixing up a batch of those scrumptious cookies. I squeezed the bottle, *which I thought was clogged,* right over the cookie dough bowl. Wouldn't you know, it suddenly opened, and Elmer's glue became an unwelcome new ingredient. Holy shit, was I in trouble!

I'm not sure if I was ordered to the corner or got spanked that time. Either way, the lesson was clear: food would *not* be wasted. I'm surprised they didn't make me eat some of the dough to prove a point. I would have!

We didn't go out to eat often as money was tight. When we did, for some dumb reason, we weren't allowed to order breakfast food for dinner. I think that's why, as an adult I love breakfast food for dinner. It feels like a small reward, in defiance of old rules.

After my parents divorced, life changed in general, including meals.

Quick Fixes

Once my mom was single, she became very busy, working full time as a bookkeeper while also attending school, with the goal of becoming a CPA. Our meals often consisted of Hot Pockets, which came in little cardboard sleeves before microwaving them until they were nuclear-hot. I'm sure this was healthy for us... *Not!*

Our TV dinners were cooked in the oven until the piping-hot apples became so hot, they could fry your tongue. But that way, you couldn't really tell how bad the food was, since your taste buds had been fried off. The frozen chocolate brownie, taken out of the tray before heating it, became a pre-dinner treat. When you are a young chef, dessert always comes first. Don't you think?

Summers spent at my grandparents' house were filled with delicious cookies, pies, and bowls of peanut M&Ms, strategically spaced for the taking. I have no self-control when it comes to those little colorful balls of peanutty goodness.

Just like back home, we enjoyed walking to the local convenience store to grab snacks and goodies. When we stayed at my grandma's house, we earned an allowance, and I always looked forward to cleaning and organizing her cupboards. There was something satisfying about tidying up her space—plus the cash that followed. The pantry was full of many boxes of crackers: Wheat Thins, Triscuits, and

Chicken in a Biskit, to name a few. Often, the boxes shoved to the back were past their expiration date. Occasionally, there was a surprise in the box but not like a Cracker Jack prize. When I opened the plastic bag, little moths would fly out!

My grandmother didn't like to throw anything away. Her fridge had a variety of opened jam jars, expired condiments, and other green, moldy surprises. Helping her clean out the cupboards meant I could capture some goodies to stash away for later. Canned vanilla frosting was one the best scores!

Have you ever enjoyed a poor-man's Oreo? That's what we called sandwiches of graham crackers with canned frosting in between. Oh my God, so good. Don't knock it until you try it.

My cousins and I would take these sneaky snacks to our fort in the field. The unharvested hay was perfect for our little hideaway. We tied a ribbon on a tall piece of hay, so we could locate it later. Our "freedom fort" would then be mowed over and forgotten until the next summer.

Cafeteria Conundrum

In elementary school, we were forced to take a bite of each type of food on our melamine tray. Main entree, fruit, veggie, and dessert, plus the little carton of milk, 2% white or chocolate. A printed menu was sent home at the beginning of each week, so you could decide if you wanted to eat the school lunch or pack your own.

The brown-paper sack containing a peanut butter and jelly sandwich, Doritos, a banana, and a thermos full of cold milk was a childhood favorite. Lunchtime felt like it came and went in the blink of an eye. Instead of enjoying my food, I usually scarfed down the contents so I could have more time with friends. My social-butterfly wings were starting to spread.

In junior high, seventh through ninth grade, we were allowed to make some choices for our lunches. Lunch A was the traditional school lunch: something premeasured from each food group, just like in elementary school. Lunch B was salad bar, where you could build your own pile of toppings with a tiny amount of lettuce underneath. Or Lunch C, where you could mix and match from among pizza, French fries, hot dogs, or a hamburger. There was the glorious other option: a Little Debbie snack cake and soft-serve ice cream. That's what I ate for lunch most days... Wouldn't you?

High school lunches were just as bad as junior high, but we also had access to snacks in the vending machines. Not only could I enjoy sugary foods for lunch, but now I could get something from the machines during the second and third passing period. That gave me ten extra minutes to fill up on overly processed, junk-filled snacks, ideal for reinforcing every student's sugar addiction... Don't get me started!

We seldom drank water growing up, except for the occasional garden hose slurp when we were playing outside. Never caring about how dirty the metal-threaded end could be. There were no reusable water bottles back then like the Stanleys or Yetis we have now. My mom drank Coke and eventually switched to Diet Coke, though I am not sure which is worse. The lower-cost off-brand soft drinks were the ones we were allowed to have. Shasta root beer suddenly comes to mind as well, along with red cream soda. I can't imagine drinking one of those now—yuck!

Once cereal became boring to me, I enjoyed strawberry Pop-Tarts, preferably with the hard white frosting on top. That is, until the next best thing was invented: Toaster Strudel Pastries, a fruit-filled pastry you cooked in the toaster. They came with individual icing packets, so you could tear off a corner and squeeze delicious frosting across the top in any decoration you pleased. Unless, of course, you had squeezed it all into your mouth while the strudel was heating and regrettably had to eat your pastry dry.

After I graduated high school and moved into my first apartment, I could eat what I wanted, when I wanted. This included late-night trips to Taco Bell and consuming raw cookie dough, spoonful after spoonful, until I threw up. Since I worked in the restaurant industry, I consumed my fair share of fried food, greasy burgers, milkshakes, and God love 'em, those darn tater tots—dipped in ranch dressing, of course!

Once I got married and our budget tightened, I started cooking more meals at home. This included a lot of Hamburger Helper, tacos, spaghetti, and pan-fried burgers. The nutritional value of our food was never a concern of mine; it was more about the cost and how quickly it could be prepared. Cooking wasn't a skill I learned growing up, as my mom was too busy making ends meet.

"Let food be thy medicine and medicine be thy food."
—Hippocrates

The Diet Dilemma

I stayed relatively thin throughout most of my younger years, largely because we spent the majority of our time outside, staying active while burning off all the calories we consumed. We didn't have the constant stream of snacks kids have today. Our meals were simple: breakfast, lunch, and an after-school snack, followed by dinner. Dessert was a rare treat.

I didn't begin to struggle with my weight until I got married and started gaining what I called the "happy fat." It came from indulging in comfort food and enjoying the happiness in my life—so I thought. Maybe that's not the scientific definition, but that is what I called it.

During my first pregnancy, my weight and food consumption ballooned out of control. The "eating for two" theory was alive and very well fed. My cravings made me hunger for macaroni and cheese, potato chips, and all the salty things. I gained fifty-five pounds, which started my yo-yo dieting phase, and I hated what I saw in the mirror.

After my daughter, Megan, was born, I was fortunate to be a stay-at-home mom. The days went by fast, and before I knew it, she was crawling all over and getting into everything. You would think chasing a baby around the house would be enough movement to shed a few pounds. Between picking up toys, running after her little legs, and constantly being on my feet, it felt like I should have burned calories from chaos. Apart from the seven pounds of her weight that I lost when she was born, though, I really struggled with getting the scale to move.

As my husband's enlistment ended and our return home came closer, I was excited to be reunited with my family and the old friends I'd grown up with. But my high school body didn't exist anymore. For God's sake, I thought to myself, I can't go back there looking like this.

> *She has a beautiful baby girl, but the number on the scale consumes her. She feels selfish about having these feelings when she has others relying on her. What she repeats to herself in the mirror are words that no mind should hear. "You look ugly." "You're fat." With no knowledge of true nutrition and without the energy to do any physical activity, she becomes desperate for a solution. And just like that, it appears.*

My first and worst diet to tackle these issues was the No-Fat Diet. *Good Morning America* was my favorite show to watch while we ate breakfast. When you have no cable television, only an aluminum-foil wrapped antenna, the options are limited. One morning, *GMA* featured a doctor who proclaimed that dietary fat was bad for your health. He suggested a fat-free diet to shed the excess pounds.

This piqued my curiosity. I was eager to learn the secrets of this transformational way of eating, and I needed it badly! Eat no fat, lose weight, and bam! Your high-school body will return... Easy-peasy, lemon squeezy. At least, that's how I interpreted it.

I immediately restocked my fridge and pantry with fat-free mayonnaise, fat-free cheese, tuna, and SnackWell's, a new brand of boxed cookies with no fat that tasted delicious. I nailed this new way of eating as I was determined to transform my post-baby bod.

I lost twenty pounds in two months, but little did I know what was happening inside of me. I hadn't lost all my pregnancy weight, but my body had regained a shape I could recognize. As our much-anticipated return home approached, I felt physically ready. When you read the Gut Monster portion of this book, though, you will hear more about the negative aspects of this fat-free diet.

A few years after we returned to Kansas, I briefly tried the Atkins Diet, which involves eating lots of fat and no sugar or carbs. There was a lot of marketing around packaged foods that were labeled "Atkins approved," so I leaned into buying and eating those, instead of whole foods. What once was a good idea turned into a cash grab. These packaged foods contained lots of chemicals and fillers to make them taste good without having any carbs or sugar. My first diet-wired my brain to think *all fat* was bad, so I didn't commit to Atkins like I probably should have.

Then came the good old Weight Watchers. Even my grandma went back and forth on this one. To me, the counting of points and tracking the food became exhausting. It seemed like a good concept, though, and I observed many others on the diet learning to eat better and smaller portions. But this was a system I didn't have time for. Then, of course, there was new marketing around convenience products they'd developed. Weight Watchers packaged meals were introduced, full of sodium and who knows what else. For me, that program went to hell in a handbasket after that. They should have kept it simple.

HCG shots then became the rage. Human chorionic gonadotropin is a hormone produced by the placenta when you are pregnant. As a diet tool, it helps you feel no hunger, and it is combined with severe diet limiting to 500-800 calories a day. I did not want to take shots prescribed by my doctor, but I was elated when I learned my chiropractor offered HCG sublingual drops. I trusted him and gave it a try.

I lost a lot of weight quickly, but, of course, when I quit the drops, I gained it back just as quickly. No one ever mentioned the importance of physical activity or working out in addition to any of these weight-loss and diet programs. It was more about the quick fixes. Obviously, I was missing a piece of the puzzle.

As the wellness industry blew up, various shakes and supplements became the new rage, including pills, teas, powders, and fillers. Protein is wonderful, but all the other stuff they add to shakes, etc., is nonsense. I dove into a few network marketing programs for products that offered the promise of rapid weight loss with little effort. Believe it or not, I gained weight with one protein powder! It was made with soy protein, and it triggered my body into thinking I was pregnant. Soy can do that to women, because it contains isoflavones, a type of plant estrogen (phytoestrogen). Even my boobs got sore!

The next thing I undertook on my weight-loss quest was more of a food plan than a diet. Raw vegan eating became a pivotal program for me, a fork in the road that led me to research health and fitness and its effects on my weight and my ultimate Gut Monster aka Crohn's disease. (I dive into this more in detail later.) In this diet, nothing is cooked at a temperature above $115°$, therefore none of the nutrients in food are destroyed by excess heat.

Another exciting thing that grew out of the raw-vegan food plan was a passion for trying new recipes. My husband supported my new way of eating from the start, and he bought me a huge dehydrator. This diet requires lots of food prep, so I began to do meal planning for the first time.

The challenge of making something taste good while still being healthy bloomed into my new hobby. Faux tuna became an instant favorite; believe it or not, it is made from dehydrated nuts. Like most Crohnies (people with Crohn's disease), I had issues digesting nuts, but I could snarf this down and still feel great! Ever since, my kitchen has remained one of my Zen zones, as it feels therapeutic.

I started working out at home as my local gym was a place I donated to monthly but never stepped foot in. Another crazy thing happened—my periods stopped! Halleluiah, right? At first, I thought this was a positive side effect from working out and eating this way, but it really wasn't. I was only thirty-eight at the time, and despite being thrilled that Aunt Flo had left my life, I now know that early menopause can cause early bone density loss and increase a woman's risk for heart disease and stroke. (Per "Menopause Basics" at www.womenshealth.gov).

What if I'd wanted more kids? Never mind… That didn't occur to me. Thankfully, I had minimal night sweats and other perimenopausal symptoms. To this day, I have never taken any hormone replacement therapy (HRT), even though it is often recommended for people in various stages of life. The idea of synthetic hormones never felt like the right choice for me.

Once on this raw-food plan, I also stopped seeing my GI doctor, as I was ready to take control of my health. You will read later how this was an enormous victory in my battle of the gut… Or was it? My research during this time set the stage for a lifelong desire to know more. After six months of eating this way, the time-consuming food prep, coupled with a lack of variety in my meals, began to bore me. So, I started to cook my food; gradually, I added animal protein back into my diet, along with other foods.

Through my ongoing research, my next favorite topic became *gluten*. That brought me to the book, *Wheat Belly*, which convinced me to remove wheat and other gluten (products also made with rye and barley) from my diet. It causes lots of inflammation. That is what Crohn's disease is: an inflammatory bowel disease. So, I adopted gluten-free flour, gluten-free this, gluten-free that.

Cauliflower replaced traditional pizza crust, and I used spiralized zucchini for noodles. I dug up a whole set of new, fun recipes and really loved using my Vegetti. (I know what you are thinking! Get your mind out of the gutter. I am not talking about vibrators again! This is a spiralizing tool used for vegetables.)

By now, I knew that eating gluten-free was far more valuable than buying ultra-processed GF products. I steered away from these unhealthy, convenient options as much as possible.

> *She is made fun of whenever eating out, as she announces her gluten-free status to the waitress. She eats in a way that most can't imagine. Her healthy self knows she is doing something good, so she persists among the hecklers. She is way ahead of the curve with this one.*

Reading the back of labels for nutritional information became my new pastime. It motivated me to include clean eating information in the Facebook groups I led for women seeking help to lose weight. I educated myself and, subsequently, others on how to swap this for that, to lower consumption of unhealthy ingredients.

This research led me to discovering the Paleo method. It involves eating lean meat, vegetables, fish, fruit, eggs, nuts, seeds, and plenty of healthy fats (avocados and olive oil); it involves cutting out processed foods, corn, soy, dairy, most sugar, and wheat from your diet. This became my new way of eating.

I used Google to discover recipes, rather than cookbooks, because I could simply add the word "paleo" when I searched for new ideas. I could eat most vegetables plus low-sugar fruits and used coconut sugar for baking. Coconut sugar is lower on the glycemic index than refined sugar which means it doesn't raise your blood sugar so quickly. (Per "Is Coconut Sugar Good for You?" at *Health.clevelandclinic.org.*) Medjool dates were also a great natural treat for my sweet cravings. Boiling them down made a delicious caramel sauce.

Even though alcohol does raise blood sugar, I continued to drink it. But when I learned it was important to consume fewer carbs, I adjusted my beverage of choice to be vodka or tequila. Skinny margaritas became my new love. When I went out for Mexican food, I brought my own veggies to eat in place of chips. Corn is used to fatten cows, and Lord knows that didn't meet my objective, so celery had to do. Rice and beans I had never enjoyed, so that was no biggie to give up.

At this point, I felt like I had gained some control over my eating habits. For several years, I ate this way and lost weight, so I began to like what I saw in the mirror. Of course, paleo became a victim of the processed food craze, too; many things started to be labeled "paleo," but they sadly included other processed ingredients.

The ketogenic diet was the next one in line. This was low carb, no sugar (not even coconut sugar), high fat, and lots of protein. If the food you ate had fiber, you could subtract that number from the carbs to measure your daily net carbs. It seemed easy enough until the keto flu hit me, a few days in. It felt like the seasonal flu with aches and pains, fogginess, and no desire to get out of bed. My body was adjusting to being fat-adapted.

When you limit your carbohydrate intake to twenty carbs or less a day, you go into *ketosis* and start to burn the fat from your body as fuel, instead of using carbs for energy. The flu associated with it lasted about a week, but after that, I had tons of energy! I became a fat-burning machine.

I purchased pee-on test strips to see if my body was producing ketones, and boy, I sure did. Unfortunately, keto also became a victim of the processed-food industry. Everything keto hit the shelves and another cash grab was born.

Like paleo, I ate this way for several years. I kept my weight off, and I felt pretty darn good. The low-carb alcohol drinks were still in my life, but wine also crept in more and more, and it has quite a bit of sugar. After years of trying different food plans, I really learned how certain food affected me, but for some reason, I did not connect the dots to alcohol, until later.

> *Her body image improves, but some of her mindset is still wrong. The Alcohol Monster morphs into a demon and makes what she sees in the mirror change. She feels ugly again, and the ruminating thoughts consume her. The pounds slowly return, raising the scale, despite the efforts of eating better and working out daily.*

> "The best advice is to avoid foods with health claims on the label or, better yet, avoid foods with labels in the first place."
> —Mark Hyman

Fork in the Road

My next step wasn't about following another diet. It was about improving my mindset around discipline and for overcoming my physical and mental obstacles. I desperately needed this.

I heard about something called the 75 Hard Challenge from my clean-eating groups and other online social media in the health and fitness world. It interested me *but* you could not consume alcohol while participating. Therefore, I opted out!

Several months later, some friends decided to do the challenge. We watched as they followed all the daily tasks involved, and they felt amazing. Mark and I decided to try this, ourselves. The founder of this challenge is a hard-core dude; I reference his book in the Weapons section later.

The food part of the challenge was to pick one way of eating and stick to it for seventy-five days—no cheating! Intermittent fasting was something I had been playing around with and doing research about, so we made that part of our plan. We fasted sixteen to twenty hours a day, breaking our fast with a high-protein snack in the afternoon, followed by a protein and veggie dinner plus the occasional almond flour biscuit. The keto-copycat Red Lobster cheddar garlic treats became a new recipe staple in our house.

Other aspects of the challenge included two forty-five-minute workouts. One had to be outside, no matter what the weather—rain, snow, sleet, or tornados. We walked in ten-degree temperatures through a foot of snow at times.

Drinking a gallon of water daily was one of the most daunting tasks in the challenge, especially when we traveled to Arizona during our seventy-five days. We had to make frequent roadside stops for urination, but we did it: if we didn't drink every single ounce every day, we had to start the challenge over. There was no way I would fail at this.

We completed our challenge on April 25, 2022, and it turned out to be undoubtedly the best and hardest thing I have ever done. It is designed as a mental challenge, but of course, you can lose weight and gain a ton of confidence in yourself, at the same time. We needed that. Between the two of us, we lost fifty pounds. The before and after pictures are incredible. (I go into more details of this later, in the Alcohol Monster section. That's where it gets good!)

After the challenge, we continued our healthy habits, but as always, I kept my eyes peeled for ways to improve. Eventually, sugar and grains made their way back into my diet, because I had not gotten rid of my real cravings. The *Dirty Keto* movie was recommended by a friend who knew I happened to be a food junkie. After I watched this documentary, I realized I had been swapping out one bad thing for another. Sugar had been replaced by stevia; and almond flour became my new flour. But many of these are highly processed and full of carbs. They may have been better options, but I was still not addressing the real issue.

I turned my attention to eating more protein again and started to include more protein powders and other supplements in my diet. But I didn't like the way it showed up on the scale, plus, I felt bloated and bulky.

FINDING HER

A friend of mine had been eating only meat for a few years, and I thought she had gone crazy. Since my first fat-free diet, I'd been convinced that fat made you fat; so, I had long denied myself things I love, like butter and red meat. But as social media algorithms began to lead from my searches, the carnivore diet started to emerge in my feed.

This way of eating eliminates everything but animal protein. No fruit, nuts, vegetables, grains, or sugar... Not even spices; only salt for flavor. So simple! As I started to dive into this food plan, I grew to understand why and how it worked.

Ironically, I had recently had blood work done, and everything reported back great except my iron. It was low, and this carnivore diet would certainly help address that. Mark and I decided to give the carnivore diet thirty days.

Then, I dove deeper in that community by watching YouTube videos from doctors and other specialists. Dr. Ken Berry, Dr. Anthony Chaffee, and Dr. Robert Kiltz are some of our favorites. When I looked for new recipes, I found Courtney Luna's cookbook, *Carnivore in the Kitchen*.

Experiencing the keto flu again wasn't fun, but I knew there would be a light at the end of the tunnel. Eight months later, we are still focusing on animal proteins and clean eating. I have finally broken free of the "diet" world. I eat mostly protein but have an occasional treat or splurge on special occasions. A new clean favorite is homemade coconut ice cream with espresso powder and cinnamon. Don't knock it until you try it!

> *She knows she has defeated some of her bad habits, but why do they creep back in after she's been doing so well? Her desperate search for answers leads her back to the beginning,*

where this Monster started. Is it really the food? Or something more? Now that her other Monsters are fading, it becomes evident and starts to make sense. Her constant battle with food centers around the scale and the mirror, not her health.

Fatty Findings

I am sure you are wondering what makes this style of eating so different from all the other diets I tried. Believe me, those questions still ruminate in my mind, as well. I could go on for days about our broken food system, but I will share some key points about how this animal-based eating has worked for us. The coach in me feels the need to.

The most significant factor is we have eliminated so many foods, seasonings, and additives from our daily life that, if we consume a food item our body doesn't agree with, we know it the next day and can pinpoint it. I believe the struggle most people have, when trying to figure out what food is triggering allergies, gut issues, skin irritations, etc., is the overwhelming task of narrowing it down. Food logging is a pain in the ass, but often it is the best way to find these things out.

Another reason we have eliminated fruits and vegetables is that what we buy in this country is so nutrient deficient, plus usually genetically modified to be bigger and sweeter. The berries I used to pick with my grandma were one fourth the size of the ones they sell in the stores today.

We now buy our grass-fed beef from local ranchers and our organic eggs from the lady with a chicken coop down the road. Of course, we still go to the grocery store to buy other proteins, but we are very careful not to purchase farm-raised fish or non-organic chicken.

On the *very* rare occasions when we go out, we try not to eat anything fried. The seed oils used in restaurants are poison to our bodies. Just last week, we tried a few pub chips at a restaurant, and the next morning, Mark and I both had puffy eyes and aches and pains in our joints.

We are still consuming dairy, but we study the labels closely. Over time, I have realized I can only tolerate it occasionally, as it leaves me feeling bloated. It's crazy how many additives they can sneak into our sour cream, cottage cheese, and heavy whipping cream. I dare you to try to find a cream that doesn't have carrageenan or guar gum in it. These ingredients are used as thickeners, and they cause lots of digestive stress. Carrageenan was something I discovered when I oversaw my clean-eating groups, as it wreaked havoc on a few of my clients' guts.

Am I worried about cholesterol? Nope. Did you know that when statins (prescription drugs prescribed to lower people's levels of LDL or "bad" cholesterol that causes plaque to build up in arteries) started to be prescribed more often, there was a huge increase in the incidence of Alzheimer's and dementia? (See "Statins" on *My.Clevelandclinic.org/health/treatments.*) Thanks, but I will pass on that.

Did you know that seventy percent of our brain is made of fat? I stumbled upon this fact years ago, while researching my disease. My mind is now clearer than it has been in years. That is one of the first things we noticed, after starting the carnivore diet. Recalling facts and trivial information seems to come to us more quickly. The brain fog we weren't aware of having until now has lifted.

Do I miss some foods? Of course. But I am now in tune with what my body doesn't like, so that makes resisting shitty food so much easier. The number on the scale is misleading, since I am gaining so much muscle, and I am happy with how I feel, which is what's important! And my clothes fit so much better! Don't get me wrong, I do still get on the scale occasionally, but it doesn't define who I am.

The simplicity of eating this way has given us more time to enjoy other things we love. Also, recipes are easy! I currently have pork chips in the oven, since I still love crunchy, salty snacks. I put frozen pork loin, thinly sliced and salted, into the oven and let it cook for about five hours. *Bam!*-Homemade protein chips! You can do the same with ground beef and other meats. We use a frozen meat slicer we purchased from Amazon. It looks like one of those old paper cutters we used in school.

What works for me may not work for you. I am not talking solely about the losing weight; I'm referring to the mindset around it, as well. *Carnivore* makes sense to me now. Will that change? It could, as new research comes around at the speed of light. Sometimes, it's hard to keep up with all of it.

As our bodies and lifestyles evolve, so do our nutritional requirements. I love eating whole, protein-based foods with minimal processing. If I choose to eat fruits or veggies, I choose something low in sugar and carbs. Remember what the vegan diet did to my period!

Now that I am eating for the right reasons, I can see the lessons each diet has taught me. The one thing they all have in common is, once they became marketable, convenient, and *very* profitable, they became unhealthy. I am angry at our food system and worry about our future generations. Americans are consuming so much processed crap, they have a very good chance of being diagnosed with diabetes someday. Just look at our children. Many are overweight, consistently sick, and taking medications sooner than ever. The hormones they are pumping into our meat is causing our girls to go into puberty earlier and earlier.

Rant over. Now I am going to go enjoy a juicy steak for dinner.

> "I am beginning to measure myself in strength, not pounds. Sometimes in smiles."
> —Laurie Halse Anderson

Monster 4

The Mirror

I INITALLY THOUGHT THE Food Monster belonged in this chapter, as a part of my Mirror Monster. But, as I gathered and wrote down my thoughts, I uncovered new insights. I have realized that the real struggle was about being at peace with my *reflection* not what I shoved in my mouth.

Early Bloomer

My early-onset puberty gave me horrible pains in my bones. It felt like my bones were being stretched to the point of being ripped apart. The discomfort was so unbearable, my parents took me to the emergency room on several occasions. I was diagnosed with growing pains; the stretch marks on my legs are a forever reminder of this phenomenon.

My boobs were part of this spurt, too. By sixth grade, I was five foot three and wore a C-cup bra. There is a picture of me wearing roller skates at that age, and I looked like all legs and tits. My awkward body brought on many nicknames from the neighborhood boys-remember the "Dolly Parton" one?

> *She is happy to have these new breasts but has no idea it will be the start of a lifelong struggle with her disproportionate body. The attention she receives fuels the Mirror Monster, as well as the Men Monster, as time goes on. Her self-worth becomes connected to her physical appearance.*

I can see evidence of my growth spurt in my sixth-grade school pictures, including puffiness in my face. Or maybe that was just the bad perm! Short curls didn't do anyone justice, nor did most of the hairstyles back then.

When I entered junior high in the early eighties, I squeezed my ass into Jordache jeans. My mom actually taught me this technique. We would lie on the bed, sucking in our guts, and then attempt the zip up, praying we didn't catch any skin. I always felt stiff as an ironing board when I tried to stand up after that. Next, a few quick squats to loosen them up, just enough to walk. Did you ever partake in this horrible ritual?

Along with this fashion trend, we were layering turtlenecks and wearing Polos with a popped collar under a sweater to create the "preppy" look. Speaking of sweaters, do you remember the song and dance we used to do to make our boobs grow? "We must, we must, we must increase our bust..." Well, let's just say, I should have opted out of that exercise.

As I began to figure out my identity, I did not embrace the preppy look for long, and my taste turned to more of a rebellious look. Rock and roll concert T-shirts were often paired with the painted-on jeans accompanied by a bandana tied around my ankle. Oh, dear Lord, those were the days!

The Distorted Reflection

What I saw in the mirror really took a turn when I first noticed the changes in my pregnant body. My boobs seemed to be growing daily, or so it felt, and my stretch marks had spread to my midsection. The fifty-five pounds I gained looked like five hundred in the mirror. Where had I gone? To a fun house or hell? I think it soon became the latter.

As you read in an earlier chapter, this was a stressful time for me, and my body seemed the bearer of the bad news. After I lost some of the weight from my first pregnancy and had started to feel somewhat better about my image, I was ready for pregnancy number two. But I was *not* prepared for another dramatically modified physique. Thankfully, I didn't gain as much weight during that pregnancy—only thirty-five pounds. I had learned a lesson from the first.

> *She feels overwhelmed by the physical weight and size of her large boobs. Her reflection shifts, and the physical road map of her life begins to take shape whenever she looks in the mirror. Her voice of reason for why this is happening is ignored as the Monsters take over. The repeated mantras are pure evil. Food will be the way she can control her image. It isn't about her health; it appears to be in vain.*

Finding time to take care of myself with two toddlers became a challenge. My first attempt at working out was at an aerobics class that had a daycare for the girls. I would do the grapevine dance move along with my girlfriend, who had children as well, and we would crack up as we tripped and tried to get in sync. This was much-needed girl time, but I didn't stick with it. I had unrealistic expectations, and my enthusiasm faded quickly when the scale didn't move. Loading the kids up and driving across town was a daunting task. Excuses, excuses, excuses!

When I began to work in the bar business, my body proved to be a valuable asset. Big tits equaled even bigger tips. No, I didn't work as a stripper! Maybe I should have, though? Nope, not a good dancer!

I did enjoy the attention and looked good with clothes on. Underneath, though, I felt ugly and would shy away from mirrors when I undressed. When it came to having sex, I would get anxious, so no lights were allowed, and the covers were pulled up to my neck.

> *She becomes afraid of the real her being exposed. The scale, the food, and the mirror are all interconnected. Scars, hanging belly fat, and sagging boobs are proof that she isn't worthy of any real love. The appearance in the mirror blinds her. She can't see the real her anymore—she is gone.*

The girls were getting older, and the newfound flexibility in my day allowed me time to join a gym. Did you notice I didn't say, "go to the gym"? I was constantly in and out of membership contracts, wondering why my body wasn't changing with each monthly payment I made. The excuses mounted, and eventually I realized working out was not something I was interested in doing.

As my mid-twenties arrived, so did losing weight with no effort. At first, I started out being happy that the scale was moving, but as time went on, I also developed horrible cramping and diarrhea. That joy turned into sadness upon the diagnosis of Crohn's disease, which exponentially changed everything in my life, especially my self-image. I looked skinny in some parts, but the inflamed belly made me look six months pregnant again. Going to the gym was not an option for me, because my unexpected bowel explosions were something I needed to stay close to home for.

> *It seems, as soon as one hangup has been resolved around the Mirror Monster, then comes another defeating blow. She tries to focus on healing and not be confused by the distorted image she sees, but her self-worth declines as fast as her health.*

I explored new prescription medications, but each one was accompanied by strange side effects. The worst meds, the steroids, turned my face into a Cabbage Patch Kid, plus I became a raging bitch! Nothing made me happy, and little things would set me off like a rocket. One of my many rounds of prednisone added forty pounds to the scale. As I tapered off the meds, I assumed the weight would disappear, as well. Not so much! I was back to battling the scale once again.

After years of trying different medications, I began to feel better and immersed myself in research about my health or lack thereof. This triggered my desire to find the perfect workout. Treadmills and NordicTracks were definitely not my cup of tea; they seemed boring and monotonous, plus I didn't have room for big equipment. Thankfully, I was introduced to Beachbody and the thirty-minute workout called "The 21 Day Fix." You just needed some dumbbells and a little space. Not only did this program guide me through a quick workout, but it helped me dial in my food portions, too. After just a few weeks of consistency, I began to see my image changing.

As cell phones advanced, so did my love for before and after pictures. They allowed me to see the progress in a different way. I was gaining control, I felt, but there were so many permanent changes to my body from prior pregnancy weight gain, I still felt unsatisfied despite all the work I was doing. I could not overlook the hanging skin that flopped over my bikini line, called an "apron"; many women have these, after giving birth. Lucky us.

> "The Monsters of the Mind are far worse
> than those that actually exist."
> —Christopher Paolini

Warrior Scars

The idea of permanently changing my body became a possibility, given changes in my financial situation, so I shifted my research to looking for an answer to this ridiculous apron thingy. A tummy tuck could be the perfect solution, I discovered.

I interviewed a few doctors and went with the most affordable one. My recovery was rough, though, because they sliced into the muscles in my abdomen. I was happy with the results. My belly button had to be reconstructed, so my sun tattoo around it now fell lower on my belly. But I didn't care; it could be hidden under a swimsuit, along with my surgical scar.

After I recovered, I slowly returned to my workouts. My pants fit better, and I stood a little taller, since my body was better proportioned. The one drawback was that my boobs looked bigger, since my waist had shrunk.

As she adjusts to the new roadmap on her belly, the mirror seems friendlier but is not forgotten. Her self-esteem has the boost she needs, for now.

One day, while cleaning the house, something on the TV caught my attention. Dr. Oz had become a favorite of mine, and the topic of the day was skin cancer. The oncologist on the show described what basal cell carcinoma looked like, and I stood there, shocked. *I* had a small, red, scaly spot on my cheek that never seemed to heal completely, and it had been there for a few years. It looked just like the picture they shared. *Shit!*

A dermatologist was the one type of doctor I had not been to, but I took that as a sign that the time had come. They scraped my cheek and sent it off to the lab. Why on Earth does it take so long to get results for these things? The waiting was torture! The biopsy results finally came, and they confirmed what I had suspected after watching the doctor on TV: skin cancer. I'm sure it didn't help that, in high school, we used baby oil to bake our bodies in the sun, while waiting for the Sun-In we'd sprayed in our hair to turn us blonder. My tanning bed visits had been a bad idea, as well.

A small surgery was scheduled to remove the cancer cells. The surgeon cut me open, removed a chunk, and sent me back out to the waiting room while they reviewed the results for clear margins. If there were still signs of cancer, they had me return to the surgical room to remove more. This went on all afternoon.

As they cut more, I worried more. Finally, we had clear margins, and he sewed me up. He then explained that, due to the depth of the cancer, they had had to make a long incision, so I didn't have a hole in my cheek. When I got in the car and looked in the mirror, I saw a bandage that went from my lower jaw to my eye. *Holy shit!*

Tears fell from my eyes like a rainstorm while Mark tried to reassure me that now the cancer was gone. A week later, I found myself back in the doctor's office for the big bandage reveal, and I could see what I'd feared was clearly true.

> *The tears stream over her incision as she looks in the mirror. Her life roadmap is not only on her body now, but also on her face. She now feels scarred for life.*

I knew from past surgeries that my skin did not heal well. In high school, my appendix burst, back in the days before laparoscopic surgery. That scar thickened and never looked right until it was removed by my tummy tuck. My facial scar was no exception.

When I returned to the surgeon, he agreed. My scar was one of the worst he had seen. Oh, lucky me! He agreed to do a complementary procedure to soften the thick line. Thankfully, that did help somewhat, but, twelve years later, I still have a very wide, white scar on my cheek. When I am asked what happened, I tell them I was in a ninja fight, and you should see the other guy. I really don't notice it in my mirror, though, unless I turn my head.

Tan Lines

Mark and I began spending weekends at the lake, which meant much of the day was spent in swimsuits, drinking the day away. The saying, "Tan fat looks better than white fat," was often repeated as we soaked in the rays.

I never liked the way I looked in a one-piece bathing suit; my boobs needed much more support to show where they ended and my waist began. My comical-sounding bra size had become thirty-six long. Most of my friends were in bikinis, so they gave me the confidence to wear one, as well, until I saw a picture of myself. I looked overstuffed and puffy, holding my twenty-four-ounce Yeti filled with a cocktail.

> *Why does it feel like everyone else seems okay with how they look? Do they have the same thoughts about her? The alcohol provides relief from the person she sees in the mirror. What lies ahead develops into another image she isn't ready for.*

My Crohn's disease symptoms began to reappear, and the energy it took from me, prevented me from working out. Despite my eating very little, I began to look six months pregnant, once again. My disproportionate body returned.

I had no time even to look in the mirror before things really went to hell in a handbasket, fast. There was the devastating news of my much-needed surgery, and that was followed by another blow! I would require an ostomy bag to permit my bowels to heal after the procedure.

My weight began to drop, so my cheeks were sinking in, and I looked like death. I weighed only 110 pounds at this point, and I had to face the reality of more scars plus having a poop bag hanging from my abdomen. How the hell would I wear a swimsuit then?

> *The road map on her body is rerouted once again. She tries to wrap her head around what the mirror will look like after surgery. Denial and depression are hard at work, and her sadness persists in silence.*

After surgery, the fabulous news of no ostomy bag was just what I needed to turn things around. As I recovered, basking in the joy of the successful surgery, I decided it was time to get fit again. The scars from the scalpel confirmed the warrior within me: I had a major victory under my belt. My attention now turned to what the age of fifty brings.

"I feel that it is healthier to look out at the world through a window than through a mirror. Otherwise, all you see is yourself and whatever is behind you."
—Bill Wither

Covid Mid-Life Crisis

I turned fifty in April 2020… Oh, what joy—*not!*

Covid restrictions royally screwed that up. I had to cancel my two-week dream vacation to Norway and the Mediterranean that was supposed to include time in Portugal to celebrate my big day with Spanish wine. That made me so sad, as the pandemic did for all of us.

The mirror was something I faced more often as I spent all that new time at home. Even though I had committed to working out, between lockdowns and the consumption of more alcohol and food, my body shifted.

I think all our bodies took on a new shape during this time. My tits seemed bigger than ever, and I developed a strange handful of fat on my sides. How do one's boobs keep growing? It does happen, they say. My weight had gone up due to the stress, but this was something more.

> *As she looks in the mirror, she sees many scars and imperfections. This isn't what bothers her now. It is another issue of disproportion she sees. Part of the Mirror Monster has been put to rest, but her true battle still lies ahead.*

After the restrictions were lifted, I knew it was time for some self-care. I began getting regular facials at the local spa. One day during my visit, the esthetician and I were chatting about her upcoming boob reduction. I had no idea there was another part of their business: a plastic surgery center. She said that doctor was one of the best.

My boobs had grown to a 32F. Bras were extremely hard to find, and my shoulders were feeling the weight. Driving home, the thought of reducing these Dolly Parton jugs made me excited. I was sure this could help me like what I saw in the mirror. Plus, clothes would fit better; bras would be cheaper, and I could buy them from a "normal store" like Target or Walmart.

Mark agreed that a consultation with the doctor seemed like a good idea. The thought of more scars didn't concern me. I had grown accustomed to seeing those. Plus, I had this strange midriff fat, so I decided to talk to the doctor about that, as well. Why not, right?

At the consultation, we discussed the reduction procedure and costs. Insurance wouldn't pay unless I had years of documentation from chiropractors and doctors regarding the breast size affecting me. That was not an option I was willing to wait for.

Next, I asked him about this strange extra weight I carried around my sides. I was ecstatic to hear him reply, "We see a lot of this from people who have had prior tummy tucks that weren't done properly."

Oh shit, I thought. What happened fifteen years ago during that procedure?

He explained that my original incision should have wrapped around my sides, but instead it had stopped at my hip bones. It was a medical term called "puppy dog ears." My decision, years ago, to go with the least expensive doctor had come back to haunt me.

> *She knows something isn't right with how her body looks. The reflection is so deceptive; therefore, it makes her question everything she sees. The Money Monster has her dealing with repercussions from when she chose the cheaper doctor years before.*

The doctor announced that both surgeries could be done simultaneously, and if all went well, I would go home the same day. That news surprised me, but I was all for it as I hated hospitals and would much rather recuperate at home. My mom came to town to help with my recovery, as moms seem to be the best nurses. Not that Mark wasn't awesome, but there is something about having your mom there for healing that makes everything better. She would help make meals and, most important, keep me from doing too much, since I am not one for lying around, napping.

My chest was slashed open, nipples moved, and my sides cut open to remove all the fat that had collected in weird places. Surgery didn't scare me, since I had been under the knife many times in the past. The doctor said it went well, so I headed for home afterward.

The anticipation of the follow-up office visit consumed me. At that appointment, the next week, they would unwrap my bandages and reveal the new me. Wow, you should see the before and after. Lots of scarring and swelling, but I finally liked what I saw in the mirror, and I looked properly proportioned.

Once I had completely healed on the outside, it was time to go on a shopping excursion. We were headed to Mexico soon, so I needed a new bathing suit and some strapless dresses. With my big old boobs, I had not been able to wear these types of clothes in the past. I found the perfect two-piece in aqua blue that covered my scars and fit great!

> *After so many years, she finally likes what she sees. Her negative body image has been laid to rest. Now, it becomes time to slay the Alcohol Monster, since the Mirror Monster has been her focus for far too long.*

"I look in the mirror and see a few scars, but I like myself."
—Steven Adler

Monster 5

Alcohol

ALCOHOL IS THE PHARMACEUTICAL of socializing. A toxic substance that is widely promoted and accepted. It blinds you from simple pleasures and mind f**** you every day. Be aware, as it can morph into a demon while you are looking the other way.

Brewing up Trouble

My earliest memories of alcohol involve family gatherings around my grandparents' pool, during our summer visits to Washington. After working in the yard, they drank a beer or two as they relaxed by the pool. No one was drunk or got out of hand.

Beer and liquor were not in our house when I was growing up in Kansas. Though most families celebrated with drinks during the holidays, my parents did not. I can't even recall seeing my dad with a beer, but he was going to school to be a pastor and alcohol was a big no-no in the Nazarene Church.

After my parents divorced, my uncle came to visit, and that became a different situation. He was a drinker, and

Mom wasn't. I remember the side of her car smeared with puke on the morning after they had visited the local Greek restaurant and consumed massive amounts of ouzo. Evidence of their good time, I guess.

After my uncle departed, a fifth of Everclear, a clear liquor, remained way up high in a cabinet. Over time, I helped dilute it by drinking some and replacing it with water, so it eventually lost its strength. Mom never knew, though, since she didn't touch it after my uncle's visit.

I was about fifteen when alcohol entered *my* life. It wasn't very hard to get my hands on it. My friends and I would steal it from our parents, like I had, or stand outside of a liquor store and ask someone to buy it for us... And many would!

One of my friends' moms drank a lot, and sadly, we took full advantage of her horrible addiction. If we paid for her six-pack, she would accompany us to the liquor store and purchase whatever we wanted. Of course, we had to drive her there, as her DUIs kept her out of the driver's seat, thank God! The legal drinking age was still years away, but that wasn't stopping me. This is when I acquired the nasty habit of smoking. I thought all the cool kids were doing it. I think the cost was less than a $1 a pack, and there wasn't much resistance to selling them to teenagers, since they were big money makers—just like alcohol.

Around the same time that both toxins entered my life, I made a new friend who lived behind our junior high. Going to her house to study after school became the highlight of my day, not to study but to drink and smoke. Her mom appeared to be a hot mess and could care less what we did, if she was even home to see what we were doing.

FINDING HER

Staying the night at her house was great: we could roam the streets without adult supervision and TP people's yards. We'd string toilet paper from the trees and bushes of her neighbors, and if it rained that night, it got soggy and stuck to everything, making it so much harder to clean up. We were so mean. The librarian lived down the street, and I swear she always had toilet paper hanging from her trees. We figured it was a payback for making us spit out our gum in the library.

I will never forget the first week of summer break when I was fifteen. I had turned into a fabulous party planner, so I thought hosting a lunchtime get together would be a great way to kick off the summer. It was also the day of a Van Halen concert.

A few of my friends brought several bottles of liquor. I think these prized possessions were Seagram's 7 and Canadian Club—*yuck*. My tummy turns just thinking about it. They had acquired this whiskey for that evening's concert, which I couldn't go to as I wasn't allowed, but why not get primed with them beforehand?

I loved that band and the singer, David Lee Roth, whose pictures were plastered on my walls. Probably pages ripped out of *Seventeen* or *Tiger Beat* magazine. During our lunchtime party, we played quarters and took shots while the radio blared, drowning out the sound of the garage door opening.

My mom had never come home for lunch… until today. Suddenly, the door from the garage opened, and kids started dispersing out the back door, grabbing what bottles they could. She screamed "What the f*** is going on here?"

I was speechless and knew I would be in deep shit, as she rarely cussed. I watched, wide-eyed, as my mom poured what remained of the alcohol into the sink. Suddenly, the shots kicked in, and the room got fuzzy. She then discovered one more cup of whiskey, so I was instructed to chug it and then go to my room.

No puking for me. I had to suck it up while I lay on the floor with the room spinning. I did learn one thing that day: I hate whiskey!

I spent thirty days in solitary confinement, or that's what it felt like. I was stuck in my room with no radio or TV. My mom was tough, and there was no early release for good behavior. Obviously, I didn't learn enough from that lesson, though, as I soon found myself in more trouble.

The plan was to have a sleepover with a friend, but as the evening transpired, I found myself in several predicaments. After I asked my mom if I could spend the night, she'd confirmed with the parents that this was okay and then drove me over there.

That night, there was a youth conference in downtown Kansas City, not far from a party we'd been invited to. This Christian-based event could be our cover-up, if we could find a ride. The parents of my friends with whom I was spending the night were going to dinner that evening, so they couldn't drive us. Instead, we politely asked elderly neighbor to give us a ride.

We packed a bag, but not with clothes. With beer, strategically obtained earlier in the week and hidden in my friend's room. He dropped us off, and we waved goodbye, acting like we were entering the auditorium. Instead, we walked down the street, where a friend's sister picked us up and took us to the party. She would also be the one to drive us home before curfew.

FINDING HER

As we drank and smoked in the upstairs room of a stranger's house, the room began to spin, and my vision turned fuzzy. I recall turning my head at one point and puking over the leg of a handsome boy I had just met. Shortly after, I left with him in his car. I'll spare you the other details, but by the time I returned to the party, all my friends I'd come with were gone, along with my ride.

I was clueless about it being way past curfew. Walking wasn't an option, since I was a thirty-minute drive away. We didn't have Uber-type ride sharing back then. I was terrified, but I had no way to get back to the suburbs, plus everyone at the house had passed out. So, I lay down and did the same.

The next morning, my friend's sister picked me up and drove me back to the place I was supposed to stay overnight. Thankfully, her mom had gone to church that morning, and she never knew I did not spend the night as originally planned.

We all felt relieved when I'd slipped past that hurdle. But then, we found ourselves in trouble when my friends' mom discovered the empty Bud Light box in the trash can. Of course, she called my mom and took me home shortly thereafter. As soon my mother saw me in my hungover state, I received orders to clean the house, top to bottom, and work off this latest bad decision. Then, I was sent back to solitary confinement.

> *Alcohol makes her brave enough to be bad and show friends she fits in. She knows these actions could land her in serious trouble, but the effects of drinking push away all those rational thoughts. She silences her with liquid courage.*

There were many pressures to drink alcohol and smoke weed when I was a teenager. If you didn't do it, you didn't fit in. My group of friends were named the druggies, at some point. That felt rebellious without my mom knowing about it. If she'd found out, she would have been disappointed, so I became expert at hiding things. Her approval was something I yearned for as a teenager, but my defiant behavior always prevented me from receiving what I desired so much.

In high school, my friends and I would pack up our wine coolers and "Cruise the Fe" on the weekends. This was the main street connecting the west and east sides of town. We would drive, while drinking, back and forth from a vacant store parking lot to the lake just outside of town and then drive back again, looking for guys and trying to find out where the party would be continued.

We didn't have cell phones, so this became the way to search for fun. If the police pulled you over, they would tell you to go around the building, pour out the alcohol, and go home. Thankfully, this never happened to me. I would have been mortified!

Many of my friends obtained fake IDs, but I never entertained the idea. It felt too risky, and I wasn't willing to go that far. I also steered away from volunteering to be the driver, since getting in trouble with the law scared the shit out of me. Add to that the wrath of my mom—no thanks!

It all seemed like innocent fun, back then. My boyfriend at the time, who ended up being Hubby Number One, was not the fun-loving drunk I was. He got jealous and angry, which kept our relationship in a constant state of chaos.

After high school, I lived in an apartment with a roommate, and parties were part of our weekend routine.

Thankfully, my roommate was a few years older that I, so getting alcohol wasn't an issue. My older coworkers were also happy to help me get the party started as well. I loved having my own place to party, since I felt like there was no judgement about what I did there. Of course, I had to hide my cigarettes, ashtrays, and booze before my mom visited, plus spray everything with Febreze.

> *At an early age, she starts to see the signs of what this Monster can do. Her boyfriend, as well as friends, experienced traumatic events in their past due to alcohol abuse, but she is too immature to interpret what that can mean for her in the future.*

Adult Beverages

Once I got married and moved to Ft. Bragg, we didn't have a liquor store hookup, until we met some friends who were twenty-one, the legal drinking age in North Carolina. Friday and Saturday nights involved beer and a game of cards with the neighbors.

Then, when I became pregnant, I cut alcohol out of my life for nine months. When my husband deployed overseas, the soldiers attempted to make alcohol there out of items they were sent by family and friends. I just couldn't convince myself this was a good idea, but my husband sure tried to. He became angry at me for not sending some of the supplies he wanted to try to distill.

My first daughter arrived a month before I turned twenty-one. After being sober for nine months, alcohol was not as desirable to me. I was a new mom, and my focus had changed.

A year later, we moved back to Kansas, where all our high school drinking friends lived. My mom was happy to have her granddaughter close by, and she became our weekend babysitter, while we reconnected with friends. It didn't take long before I concluded that alcohol, bars, and pool tables did not mix well with my jealous husband. On many evenings, I went to bed so angry and embarrassed for what had transpired during our night out. I became an expert at walking on eggshells and smoothing the waters to ease the tension, when he was involved in some confrontation.

As I continued to work in the service industry, I began to understand how hanging out in bars destroyed families. People would spend hours at the bar after work, instead of going home, to avoid family life. Since cell phones were still not common, women would call the bar, asking for their husbands. I hated the position that put me in, but it paid my bills.

The amount of money people spent at the bar blew my mind. Men would chug beer and take shots while staring at TVs and smoking one cigarette after another. I quit smoking while pregnant, but the bar environment got me hooked again. Not only did I inhale toxins from my own Marlboro Lights, but also from the twenty people who sat at my bar. The disgusting smell permeated my hair and clothes, but this felt like a small price to pay compared to the tips I made. Alcohol equated to money.

As I started making friends at the bar, I came to the realization that how I was raised, with sober holidays, was uncommon. Many of the customers had backgrounds with alcoholics, and drinking seemed to be a family affair.

Alcohol started to creep into our lives more and more. Going out to eat wasn't just for food anymore. Cocktails or beers were always involved—it was a part of the culture. Hosting people for drinks at our place helped me feel more at ease with our consumption of alcohol, and since we had a pool in the backyard, these events occurred often.

> *She again feels the need to fit in and be part of the party. The environment around her encourages drinking, so her identity becomes all about having fun. The Monsters take full advantage of this.*

Liquid Courage

After my first divorce, I drank several times a week. Mostly, when I got off work, and then during the occasional night out with friends. I wasn't someone who enjoyed drinking alone.

Then, I began dating Hubby Number Two, a customer at my bar, and I noticed my alcohol consumption started to rise. He didn't have kids, so we made the most of the weekends when my girls were with their dad. Unfortunately, his deceptive ways convinced me to leave the girls at home more than I care to admit, while going out at night.

> *Her occasional drinking turns into more than she bargained for. She knows leaving the girls at home to go out with him is not right. Her strength fades faster than ever, as the Men and Alcohol Monsters merge the day she marries him.*

Up to this point, I hadn't had the luxury of going on vacation, let alone travel outside the U.S. Mexico became my first of many all-inclusive getaways. Unlimited alcohol for the week blew my mind—Party time! I loved this idea. Not seeing all the cash that we were spending every time we ordered drinks calmed my constant worry of money.

On my first trip to Mexico, I thought, why not get my first tattoo? It sounded like a good idea, right? Well, the margaritas convinced me this was a great idea. The bright sunshine on the beach inspired the ring of sunrays I had tattooed around my belly button. Surprisingly, twenty-five years later, it still has good color on it, even after going under the knife.

We really enjoyed traveling with a group of friends. The all-inclusive trips to Mexico became a yearly event, usually in January or February, when we all wanted to escape the cold. During the summer months, we went on river float trips, camped, and took trips to the Lake of the Ozarks, which included the infamous Party Cove. This was one of the biggest, drunkest, titty-flashing parties in the Midwest. Thousands of boats tied up together, and then we all went swimming in water full of piss and who knows what else.

Alcohol was the one thing that glued this group of friends together. It's not that we didn't like one another, but that is all we did. When you hang out with people who like to drink as much as you, it makes you feel comfortable with what you are doing. When I drank, I did things the sober me would *never* have dreamt of doing. Lots of embarrassing moments.

Mark was the person in our circle of friends I felt the safest with. He was older and seemed more responsible. When we were in Puerto Vallarta, our group loved to go to a famous local Mexican restaurant that had top-notch food and tequila. Somewhere, there is a picture of me on Mark's lap, holding my chin up, while the waiter is pouring tequila down my throat. Mark's girlfriend didn't care, as we were all just having fun.

Unfortunately, it wasn't long before most of the couples we had enjoyed traveling with began to split up—including me. I found myself divorced, once again.

> *When he takes everything from her financially, she struggles with the horrible decision she made to marry him. Even though she never misses a day of work from partying with him, there is a lot of guilt, coupled with very unhealthy food choices that leave her even more tired and depressed. The beatings that began to take place in her mind on the days after are horrific.*

I started working at a Mexican restaurant known for their great margaritas. The raspberry swirl variety tasted delicious and reminded me of the Slurpees we drank as kids. The food at this place was pretty good, too, and the nightclub it transformed into became party central. There was DJs, karaoke, and dancing until 2:00 a.m., followed by after-closing shift margaritas, so I would often get back home after 3:00.

I started to date a really nice guy—easy to talk to and fun to be around. But it didn't take me long to notice something that bothered me; he drank every single day, even while at home.

> *Even though she has consumed a lot during her second marriage, she doesn't want to be with someone who drinks every day. She needs to get away from those people and find other ways to have fun. Blaming them proves easier than listening to her.*

> "The devil has never found a better tool
> in the history of the world to destroy
> the happiness of human beings than liquor."
> —Milton R. Hunter

Boozy Beginnings

Life went on as a single mom until, three years later, I married Mark. I knew he liked to drink: I was his bartender for nine years. But he seemed more mature in all aspects of life. His job was important, and he took it *very* seriously.

Our Hawaiian-themed wedding and reception at the VFW turned out to be an epic celebration, with rum punch and plenty of other drinks. Once we left the hall, we relocated the party to a local bar that had live music. We closed that place down and made a run for the border. No, we weren't going to Mexico on this honeymoon, but we did go to Taco Bell at 2:00 a.m.

After pigging out on tacos and burritos in our hotel room, we passed out. The wakeup call we were supposed to receive a few hours later did not happen. When we woke up, we realized our flight was about to depart. Holy shit balls!

As we looked around the hotel room, littered with fast food-wrappers and other evidence of the night's drunken chaos, we quickly shoved our scattered clothes into our suitcases and hauled ass to the airport. I looked like a hot mess express, with my hair glued to my head from the hairspray the night before.

We missed our original flight and had to book a new one to our port in San Juan. We were not even sure we would make it there in time to board our cruise. I am one of those people who is always early and never late, especially when it comes to a trip. But we were lucky once again: they unlocked the gangway and let us on board. Damn, that was close.

> *Drinking nearly ruins her honeymoon. At the time, she doesn't blame the alcohol. To her, it was the hotel's fault for not giving her the wake-up call. You see, while this Monster is at work, so is denial. She isn't ready to connect the dots and listen to her.*

My pocketbook (yes, I know that word dates me) did not like the cruise format, because it hated seeing the cost of all the alcohol, since it was not included. I missed my all-inclusive vacations.

After the honeymoon, life seemed good. We now had a house with a pool, which, of course, meant hosting parties like before, which I loved! The pool became another gateway to make alcohol acceptable. Plus, if we hosted, it was more relaxed—no calculating how many drinks we had or conversations about whether we were okay to drive.

Mark had a motorcycle when we got married, which gave us a reason to travel to cool places for bike rallies. Biketoberfest in Daytona Beach was my first, and it was so fun. We hauled the bikes behind a friend's Class A motorhome and partied the whole way there.

If you haven't been to a bike rally or festival, let me tell you about them. Motorcycles, bikers, vendors, slutty attire, booze, and an occasional boob or boobs. I bought my first pair of custom chaps there. I loved dressing the biker part. I felt like a kid dressing up for Halloween.

Not only is everyone drinking and riding motorcycles, but they also use handkerchiefs for helmets, better known as do-rags. Oh my God, how stupid!

Now, it was time for me to join the gang. Not like Hell's Angels, but like the group of bikers we rode around with. I went to a motorcycle riding school and bought myself a beautiful, dark-gray Harley Davidson Sportster with pink flames on the gas tank. Chrome motorcycle parts were what I received for gifts now, instead of jewelry. Diamonds aren't every girl's best friend.

Mark and I attended bike nights at our favorite biker bar. What is a bike night? An evening designated for bikers to go to a bar, look at cool bikes, and, you guessed it, drink. The private club where we were regulars served no food. You can see where I'm going with this. The only thing they served was drinks, something that impaired people who ride on two wheels while wearing a cloth on their head for protection.

> *Again, she knows it seems wrong and idiotic, but this Monster has a stronger hold on her. Even though she feels like a badass, because she feels accepted again, she remains clueless to its power. What does she want to prove? Could she be that desperate to fit in? Why does being a bad girl feel so good?*

Sturgis is one of the biggest bike rallies in the world. It takes place in South Dakota, and many of our friends attended. After I had attended a few smaller rallies, I honestly had no desire to go to this big yearly event. Something told me it would end badly. (Sadly, it really had for one of Mark's friends, a few years before we were married.)

As I gained experience with riding, we both took our bikes on smaller trips to scenic places, but I was still nervous around curves and hills. Bikers typically love those, but something inside kept me from getting comfortable.

> *When she drives her bike down the highway, she starts to see the pavement under the wheels a little differently. It makes her nervous and scared. She doesn't love this anymore. Thankfully, she hears her and sells the bike. Her gut wins this time!*

Mark still had his bike, so I went from being a driver to a passenger—more like a backseat driver. As texting and driving became more prevalent, so did motorcycle injuries and death. A couple we knew from the biker bar were hit by an impaired driver. She died, and he lost his leg. We were done. No more motorcycling for us. Mark sold his bike, and we bought a Jeep. Four wheels on the pavement felt much safer.

When my girls were younger, my parents had a lake house, and I am thankful that alcohol was not included in these family weekends. We made so many fun memories there, and because of that, I found myself yearning for something similar. This seemed like the right time for Mark and me to have our own place at the lake.

Like many people, we started off small, to make sure this was something we wanted to do. We purchased a travel trailer and rented a spot at an RV park adjacent to the lakefront bar. Just what we needed, right?

On weekends, we headed to our tiny trailer with a cooler full of food and alcohol. We would return home with much of what we brought, though, since the bar became the place where we landed for most the weekend. We did not have a boat, and just hanging out at the campground got boring real quick. Meanwhile, our unattended pool was not being used as it should. So, we sold the camper and left the lake life.

After my girls graduated high school, we spent more weekends at the lake, not with my parents, but with our friends. Many of the friends Mark worked with had second homes there. We fell in love with boating and the life on the lake. We weren't going to Party Cove like before. Things were different now... like my boobs. They were much lower and not worth exposing. Plus, we were getting older and smarter. Or were we?

As the house with the pool lost its luster, we sold it and began the process of building our dream home. This new house had a great lower-level area with a wet bar, beer fridge, and a gorgeous view of our treed lot, a perfect setting for our large deck that ran the length of the house.

It's Wine O'clock Somewhere

Our taste buds were becoming more sophisticated, so we became interested in wine. If you haven't figured out by now, I like to go all in on *everything*! Wine was no exception.

One new hobby was making my own wine. I liked how I could make a bottle for less than purchasing it. $2-7 per bottle compared to $10 or more at the liquor store. Coming up with names and gifting my home-made concoctions brought me joy. My first batch happened to be a white wine that I named Della Jane Chardonnay after my grandma. Surely, she was shaking her head in heaven, hoping I would get my shit together soon.

Now, our trips and adventures involved wineries and breweries. Mark preferred craft beer over wine, but he slowly developed an appreciation for wine, as well. Herman, Missouri, an old German town, had tons of wineries within walking distance, so it became a place we visited often.

Pairing food with wine was so much fun. Red wine with steaks and pizza, or white wine with fish. Dinners went from bars and cheap cocktails to fine dining and wine. We were drinking classier, and that felt more acceptable.

> *Denial comes in many different forms. The amount of energy, time, and money she spends on alcohol begin to bother her. The wine corks in vases around the house as décor are a constant reminder. She wants her to be heard, but she seems afraid that, without alcohol, they will have nothing in common.*

As the lake life appealed to us more and more, we decided to purchase our own waterfront cabin. We found a three-bedroom, three-bath house with a big deck and a dock. A perfect place for our weekend getaways. The family agreed. The location was close to all our friends but far from lots of boat traffic.

Alcohol was a huge part of that culture, and we felt right at home, once again. On a typical weekend, we would arrive on Friday evening and get the car unloaded. Then, it turned into cocktail time, which lasted until bedtime. The next morning started off with Baileys or RumChata® in our coffee, and then we moved on to mimosas and Bloody Marys.

Next, we'd eat some breakfast and pack a cooler filled, of course, with beer, canned vodka seltzers, and bottled water. Among our friends, the boating rules stated you always packed the cooler full, as you never knew how long you would be on the water.

Often, late lunches would wind up being at an overpriced waterfront restaurant. The "Pain in the Ass" frozen drink became one of my favorites. One side rum runner and the other, piña colada. Of course, I added in an extra shot of Bacardi 151 to make sure it tasted plenty strong. This, again, reminded me of the childhood Slurpees.

After cruising and having lunch, we would find a friend's dock or cove to sit at and enjoy our cooler contents. By the time we got back home, we were all feeling pretty darn good. Now it was time for wine, paired with steaks on the grill. Card games followed, if we weren't too intoxicated. Then, we crashed early, wiped out by the sun and the fun.

Sundays were shorter party days, since we had to go back home later that day. Some weekends, our work schedules allowed us to stay Sunday night and drive home early Monday. That gave us a full day on the water. After our company left on Sunday morning, we would head to another local watering hole (or should I say hole in the wall?) that served fried chicken and delicious frozen margaritas-to-go. Thirty-two ounces of tart tastiness to take on the boat while we soaked up the sun. After a while, these weekends became like Groundhog Day—every weekend, the same old thing.

Boating and all the components of docking, covering the boat, and cleaning it grew stressful. The snappy, judgmental attitudes caused by the day's drinking made for many grouchy evenings. I would compare it to putting up wallpaper with your spouse—not fun!

When we were back home in the city, wine became our nightly ritual at dinner. One glass would morph into drinking a bottle, which then turned into bottles. That is when boxed wine entered our lives. With the black box, you couldn't really see how much you were drinking, unless you counted how many glasses you poured. And nobody was doing that.

> *This Monster makes her feel comfortable in sneaky ways. Guilt on Monday for the consumption over the weekend festers inside her. She's had so much fun and can't wait to do it again. The weekdays are now spent focusing on getting ready to do it all over again. She can't see the beauty of the lake, as her vision is fogged. Inside, it grows, and her mind pays the toll. As the disease wreaks havoc, she now ruminates on the effects drinking is having on her body.*

My Crohn's disease had damaged my body. As a result, I had to pump it full of steroids and hydrocodone. I spent more time in bed than not. When a bowel resection loomed, my desire to drink vanished just like my health had.

Two weeks after surgery, I was back to having energy and eating normally. Our celebrations of the successful procedure included dinner and drinks. My depression around being sick started to subside, and my life started to return to normal.

Mark retired two months later, and we moved to the lake as full-timers. Six months prior, we had purchased a larger lake home, five houses down the street from the first. We loved that cove and our neighbors. This one had five bedrooms, three baths, and two garages with a shop, allowing us to entertain more family and friends and, of course, have bigger parties!

> *She grows concerned about this move. She knows what the weekend lake life looks like and is scared it will be that way seven days a week. They are celebrating his retirement, so she quiets the thoughts by reassuring her it will change eventually.*

Mark and I had just a few friends who lived at the lake during the week, so, to occupy time, we became regulars at the local Mexican restaurant, Carmelita's. Why does it feel so good to walk into a bar and have them know your name and what you drink? I imagine it's like how Norm felt on *Cheers*. Aging myself again.

> *There appears to be a sense of belonging in the world of drinkers. She starts to relate to the past regulars from the bar, years ago. Her voice grows louder, but reality is too hard to face. Daily promises to her quickly turn into more drinking to cover the shame. She has no self-control. The deep-rooted denial and sadness of being stuck with no way out consumes her.*

Why was no one else talking about this? Did my friends have the same thoughts? They were drinking a lot, as well. How would I ask without sounding like I was being judgy or condescending?

"Hey, friends, over cocktails tonight, let's chat about how drinking makes us feel…"

That would be weird. Whenever I woke up and mentioned my morning mind f***s, Mark's famous line always was, "Let's have no regrets today please."

I did do this a lot, and I am sure it was irritating, but inside, I wished to spark a conversation around consumption, since I knew quitting by myself would be hard. Still, it was easier to pop the cork and keep going. Any conversations about limiting our alcohol intake led to arguments and regrets about bringing up the topic.

In January 2020, we went on an all-inclusive trip with a close group of friends. The details of what happened aren't important, but one evening, some stupid arguments took place due to our alcohol consumption over the day. As always, on our vacations, the days were spent drinking.

> "A bottle of wine was good company."
> – Ernest Hemingway

Birthday Shots? No, Thanks!

When March arrived, we found ourselves locked down from Covid. We felt lucky, because we had the luxury of the outdoors to enjoy, but we also had fewer planned activities and more time to drink.

We didn't start our day off with cocktails, but happy hour seemed to begin earlier, and the stress of the world took its toll. My fiftieth birthday was approaching the next month, and our dream vacation to Norway became a cancellation nightmare. Even though I had purchased insurance, the process turned out to be daunting. I was downright f***ing pissed at the world!

Reading self-help books became my way to fight off the ever-looming depression that affected so many of us during this time. No one knew what life would look like after this lockdown, so I used that as an excuse to keep the booze flowing. During this time, we were working out at home. Daily walks became a part of our routine, as well. So, not all our pandemic habits were bad.

> *She appears healthy from the outside. Her love for yoga, walking, and lifting weights keeps her balanced during this time of turmoil. This Monster is hard at work, but the world's chaos keeps her mind occupied, so she doesn't see the destruction.*

Mark and I were struggling in our relationship. This is one of the harder things for me to write about now. Sometimes, he slept on the couch... Well, what I mean is, he passed out there. Many times. His personality began to change when he drank, especially whiskey.

When I saw a shift in the look of his eyes, I questioned him about his level of intoxication. He, in turn, retaliated with slurry words that left me feeling anxious about what I knew lay ahead. It wasn't as if he physically hurt me, but his new temperament turned him into someone I didn't recognize. This happened more and more, so I began to consider alternatives—like divorce. I was not ready for that, so I kept hoping for a change... for both of us.

As the world opened back up, it felt so good to reconnect with people. We had really missed dock parties, boating to our favorite swim-up bar, and vacations. Between surgery, Mark's retiring, moving to the lake, and then Covid, we hadn't traveled much. Home had turned into our destination for drinking during those times.

We began to plan trips for the following year, giving us hope that things would be back to normal. In November 2021, we traveled to Cancun for a weeklong all-inclusive vacation. This resort had been one of our favorite resorts in the past, so we assumed it would be just as fabulous. Little did we know, it would be our last.

The first night, the margaritas gave me horrible acid reflux. Choosing another liquid libation became a chore all week long. I disliked every drink I ordered. People were rude, the place wasn't clean, and the usual drinks by the pool were boring. My love for this type of vacation was fading.

> *She has never felt so sad on a tropical vacation. This used to be a place that brought her happiness, but now it brings confusion and frustration. What happened? Her voice is finally being heard, but it comes at such a strange time... Or does it?*

Sobering Truths

A month before this Mexico trip, our good friends had begun the 75 Hard Program I mentioned earlier in the book. They wanted us to start when they did, but we had this trip planned, and there was no way I was going to Mexico and not drinking. We told them we would consider it when we got back.

After the fiasco on the trip, I felt it was a sign that maybe we really needed to take a good look at our drinking and the life that surrounded it.

That's when it hit me: I had not gone longer than a few days without drinking over the past few years. This sobering truth really scared me.

As our friends were crushing the challenge, I grew jealous but proud of them for doing something so amazing. They were feeling great, losing weight, getting stronger, and not drinking! I desperately wanted to feel the same.

> *She needs this in her life, but no way she will do it during the holidays. The thought of not drinking starts to appeal to her, but she grows extremely worried about what it will do to her marriage. Realistically, though, that isn't working so well,*

either. Little does she know this paved a path that will lead her to victory.

After the holidays, Mark and I took a trip to Arizona to visit the friends who had recently completed that 75 Hard Challenge. They lived at the lake, close to us, but they were in Arizona, scoping out the area for a possible relocation.

After the challenge was over, she'd started occasionally drinking wine, but I could tell she was conflicted about picking it back up, since she had felt so much better, mentally and physically, without it. She told me, if *we* started the challenge, she would repeat it with us.

From my experience managing weight loss groups, I knew how powerful it could be to have others participating alongside you. I was excited to have her and Mark on this journey with me.

Mark and I spent a week in Casa Grande, Arizona and fell in love with the warm weather, so we purchased a tiny home and became snowbirds.

Once we got home from that visit, we agreed to start the challenge. Both of us were feeling the desire for a big shift. On February 13, we attended a dinner with family for our granddaughter's eighteenth birthday. We ordered a bottle of wine, which turned out to be our last.

The next day, we began the challenge. Valentine's Day, in my mind, became the perfect day to start. Going into it, I was anticipating some unknowns, but I kept telling myself "You can do anything for seventy-five days."

Let me list all the tasks we had to do daily.

1. Drink a gallon of water.
2. Take a progress picture.

3. Read ten pages of a non-fiction book.
4. Pick a diet and no cheat days.
5. Exercise twice a day for forty-five minutes; one of the workouts had to be outside.
6. No alcohol.

Number 3 proved to be the easiest for me, as non-fiction books are what I love to read. Our friends suggested a book by Annie Grace called *The Naked Mind*. This book is about an alcohol-free life, but it was not written by an alcoholic or someone who had participated in the infamous AA program.

While I read this book, the effects of drinking and the facts about what alcohol does to the body really smacked me in the head. The author explained how the marketing and propaganda behind alcohol followed the techniques of Big Pharma. I could relate to that, after dealing with my illness. I would read sections of the book to Mark, which annoyed him because he wanted to read it, himself. I could not wait to share what I had learned. Patience is not my virtue!

This book drastically changed my perspective on alcohol. I started to get angry at our world for fooling me into thinking otherwise. I knew I would not return to my old ways after these sober days, but at that point, I was not ready to commit to a life without alcohol. I thought, when this challenge is over, I could simply reduce my drinking to a few days a week. Truthfully, all I was thinking about was the glass of wine I would have on day 76.

Mark started the book, and when he finished, he turned to me and said, "I don't think I'm going to drink again, ever!" *WHAT?*

She thinks, "Oh Lord, how could we stay married sober?" Their lives revolve around alcohol, and she doesn't know how to do it any other way. But this makes her happy, because there have been troubles in their marriage over the past year due to this demon, and finally, he has listened to her, as well. She figures these promises of sobriety will fade, since they have never been spoken aloud before this.

A month after starting 75 Hard, we drove to Arizona to take possession of our new tiny home. Little did we know *that* would be the real challenge.

The drive was approximately twenty hours. I think we stopped every hour to pee. Then, we had to find a place to do our outdoor workout, so we booked our Airbnb next to a park. We did our other forty-five-minute workout inside the rental.

Once we arrived at our new community, we started making new friends, and most of them loved happy hour at 3:00 p.m. If we were asked about what we were drinking, we simply told people we were doing this program and couldn't drink. That was easy, since most people were intrigued by this, so it became the topic of conversation.

She feels weird, going to happy hours without alcohol. How can she loosen up and be social? Her confidence and butterfly wings are shrinking. She isn't convinced they will be AF (alcohol free) when this challenge ends, therefore she still can't see life without it.

We headed home and completed the challenge the next month. Both of us hadn't felt this good, mentally and physically, in years!

I drove Mark crazy with my constant questions about his commitment to this new way of living, since I didn't trust either one of us.

My birthday was coming up just a few days later, which made me nervous. It would be another test to our sobriety, but we passed with flying colors! This was the first time I had celebrated my birthday without alcohol in thirty years. Writing that here really put things in perspective for me. Navigating this new alcohol-free lifestyle would be our next adventure.

As spring approached, so did our annual maiden voyage out on the lake. That was when it dawned on me: this would be the first time riding in our boat without alcohol in the cooler. Now, *that* seemed strange! Would we still have fun? What would we pack?

As we tooled along the banks of the lake, looking at all the beautiful homes, something we loved to do, my mind reeled. I realized that everything we did at the lake revolved around alcohol, and I didn't want to have those pressures. Oh sure, there are people who live on the lake and don't drink, but my vision of what life would be like ahead had changed.

Our new Arizona winter life was filled with walking, working out, biking, pickleball, and golf. That was the new life I desperately wanted, every day—not just in the winter. The town we lived in at the lake wasn't conducive to that lifestyle. There were no gyms close by, and we lived on a narrow, twisty gravel road, so biking was out of the question, too. There were pickleball courts in town, but they were far away.

After a few alcohol-free boat rides to our favorite lakefront bar, we came to the sobering reality that the cost of boating wasn't worth it anymore. $60 for fuel alone and then the overpriced, unhealthy food—no thanks!

A whole new perspective started to form. Over the years, we had spent a small fortune, basically just to get to a place where we could drink, like our old biker bar. Mark and I had a serious conversation, and we concluded that this way of living had become another crutch for alcohol, just like wineries, breweries, and bars had been. It was time to move away from the lake.

The thought of selling this house made me sad, since the kids and grandkids loved the weekends there. We took joy in hosting them, as well as our friends, but Mark and I were now in a new season of our lives. We met with our realtor, who informed us the market happened to be perfect for selling. We quickly listed our home and began our search for an active community back home in the general Kansas City area.

As our vision for a new life came to us, so did the right neighborhood. A maintenance-free home on a golf course—perfect! We found a spec home and began the process of picking out all the finishings. Back at the lake, we kept busy fixing up some last-minute repairs. It sold quickly, and we moved back to an apartment in Raymore, Missouri, while we waited for our new home to be finished.

Apartment life gave us time to fill our schedules with healthy activities, such as joining the local community center that had workout classes as well as pickleball. Being near family again allowed us to spend quality time with them on the weekends—not drunk ones!

She finally makes it here to the life of her dreams, though it always felt unattainable. She has worked hard in life, and now she will take care of herself in the healthy way. Her thoughts appear much clearer, and she feels ecstatic to be free of the daily roller coaster.

This new lifestyle still has some things for her to overcome. The Alcohol Monster has disappeared, but now there turns out to be something else rattling inside. She acts confused about what to say when questions arise. People will think she has been a raging alcoholic or had a DUI. This new version is a stranger she will have to get to know. Her social-butterfly wings are getting smaller. She used to be someone who always needed others' energy to fuel her inner soul, until now. She feels lost—like a stranger within her own body.

Mocktail and Misconceptions

During our sobering challenge, it became easy to explain why we weren't tipping the bottle. We were proud to announce it. Why did it seem harder afterwards? Honestly, I grew so afraid of the dilemma of what to tell people, it made me worried I would cave and start drinking again. We chose to quit for our health and for ourselves. I replayed this in my head over and over.

"Why the heck am I making excuses when it should be the other way around?"

As time passed, the words came easier for us. Mocktails became our new happy hour treat. My bartending skills finally came in handy, for the good. The alcohol free (AF) movement started just in time for us to have choices. Yippee. Margaritas were now made with an alcohol-free tequila, lime juice, and lime seltzer, plus, of course, salt around the rim. Mark found an AF craft beer he enjoyed, and we both loved the AF Corona. You can't hardly tell there isn't alcohol in that beer.

Finding a red wine that we could pair with our steaks became our next quest. But that is the one thing you just can't replace. Believe me, I have tried. I did find some great "Prosecco"-type bubbly that is fun to drink on special occasions. Also, a yummy AF coconut rum replacement that is delicious with pineapple juice.

As we continued our happy hour transition, I realized I used to joke that my daily routine could be summed up in three drinks: coffee, water, and wine. Now, it is coffee, water, coffee, water, and then mocktails.

Mark and I were also excited about the cost savings that might come with not drinking alcohol. Unfortunately, we discovered the alcohol-free options are pricier than their alcoholic counterparts. My mind and health are worth way more!

Because we were the new kids on the block within our new golf course community, we found ourselves in these uncomfortable situations once again. At my first Tuesday night ladies' golf league, I became aware of the term "birdie juice." I hadn't golfed in years, and this wasn't in my wheelhouse, but as you can imagine, someone gets a birdie, and the group takes a shot.

All these excuses were racing in my head. Which story do I tell? Suddenly, the words just flew out: "I don't drink." The looks were subtle, but I could see their wheels turning. I cheered the team with a shot glass full of water, but it felt awkward.

It frustrated me that I couldn't find the right words. I had to remind myself I used to be one of them, not long ago. Shamefully, the words, "I don't trust someone who doesn't drink," had come out of my mouth many times during my drinking days. Such a stupid thing to say.

As we gathered some neighbors together for a block party, someone made a comment made about my AF Corona: "What's the point in drinking that, if there's no alcohol in it?"

I knew this day would come, but I didn't have the words to reply. I became speechless for the first time in my life.

I have no judgment about others who drink. Actually, I am jealous of them at times. Most of our friends still do drink, except the ones who did that challenge before we did. I now call her my sober sister and am forever grateful that she paved the way for me to fight this battle.

> *These thoughts cross her mind often. "Why can't I just have one or two, every once in a while?" and "How do they do that?" This battle is one she wasn't expecting, but she knows she can overcome it, as she grows stronger every day. Thankfully, her sober sister is there to hold her hand. They both are navigating new waters.*
>
> *This is when she starts to see her true self emerge. Who is this stranger? There are so many changes, she can't recognize her, but she likes this person. Then, she asks more of herself by reflecting and not blaming that old version.*

The desire to drink slowly eased, which boosted my self-confidence. I started to reframe the thoughts, centering them around living longer and being the healthiest I could be…, without looking back. Over time, it became apparent there were plenty of reasons why I shouldn't drink and very few for why I should.

As I write this, Mark and I just celebrated our third AF anniversary, on Valentine's Day, 2025. That is the gift I want to receive every year on this Hallmark holiday. There's no need for cards or flowers.

Waking up every day without a hangover, without feelings of guilt and shame—that is the best present we have ever given each other and ourselves. Navigating life without alcohol is now a distant memory for me, and that monster is forever slayed.

> "The day I became free of alcohol was the day that I fully understood and embraced the truth that I would not be giving anything up by not drinking"
> —Liz Hemingway

Monster 6

Gut

LIVING WITH CROHN'S disease has been a true roller coaster, marked by sudden drops and unexpected turns, with brief moments of relief between long stretches of uncertainty. It's a ride I never wanted to be on, but one that has shaped me in ways I never anticipated.

Well, Crap!

In my early twenties, I had no idea how much pregnancy, coupled with emotional eating, had changed me. I developed a food-focused coping mechanism while my husband was in the military overseas, and that resulted in massive weight gain.

Before my pregnancy, I never worried about what I ate, but trying to reclaim my pre-pregnancy body turned into a huge challenge for me. (See Monster 3: Food!)

In my first dieting attempts, as you've read, I believed fat was an enemy to avoid at all costs. In fact, the body needs fat. When I eliminated all fat from my diet in those attempts to get back to my pre-pregnancy body, I unknowingly put tremendous stress on my digestive system, which contributed to problems that were headed my way.

The role of dietary fat is to help absorb vitamins as well as to assist food as it moves down our digestive tract. With no fat, your bowels will have reduced motility. This leads to irregular bowel movements and improper elimination of your poo.

> *She assumes it is just a phase or a stress-related issue; but it quickly spirals into something that will redefine her forever. Her inner voice is silent, or maybe she doesn't know it exists. The gut instinct begins to form.*

It began not long after I had finally managed to lose some of the baby weight. At first, I didn't think much about it, but looking back, that's when everything shifted.

My first shitty memory is from when we lived in North Carolina. As we were leaving Myrtle Beach with some friends, we had to pull over so I could quickly exit the car. Not because I felt car sick, but to empty my bowels on the side of the road. I had no ability to hold it, so I figured it would be better in the ditch than in their car!

Do you know how embarrassing it is to wipe your ass with a sock along the roadside? Utterly humiliating.

These episodes were few and far between, so I didn't think much of it then.

We moved back home to Kansas, and I had my second daughter. My two toddlers were potty-trained without much trouble, but now I was stuck in a vicious cycle of bathroom visits, abdominal cramping, and urgency.

My body wasn't absorbing nutrients, and I constantly felt fatigued. As I chased my toddlers, my fuel tank was running on empty. Planning my outings became less about the destination and more about knowing where the closest toilet was located. I mapped out my life around convenience stores, gas stations, and public restrooms.

I didn't realize it at the time, but I had started losing control. And not just of my bowels. Of my freedom and my sense of self. My loose stools weren't something I felt comfortable talking to my friends about, though, and because of that, I had no idea that this was abnormal. Our chit-chat was about kids, work, marriage, and what we were cooking for dinner... Not my poop schedule. (Times were very different from today, where bowel movements are a regular topic of conversation in my circles!)

I began to log my food in and stools out, down to the color, consistency, and—I hate to even say it—the odor. The mental and physical toll was relentless. Every meal became a gamble. Would this food send me into a spiral of pain and cramping? Was it something I ate? Or just in my head? On the rare days when I felt "okay," I clung to hope, only to be blindsided by another wave of symptoms the following day. The cycle felt like a broken record: eat, cramp, double over in pain, sweat, panic, and desperately search for a toilet.

> *Her body morphs into a battleground, and her mind grows consumed with fear. She thinks, Am I going to die? Is this my life now? She has moments of panic when barely making it to the bathroom in time—or she doesn't make it at all. It overwhelms her.*

"Health is not valued till sickness comes."
—Thomas Fuller.

The Medical Merry Go Round

After a few years on this ride, I wanted off! I began seeking answers, desperate to find out what was wrong.

I made an appointment with my primary care doctor, the first step of what became a much longer journey. After explaining my symptoms, he quickly referred me to a gastroenterologist (G.I. doctor). After filling out what seemed to be a mountain of paperwork, I obtained an appointment. This became my first of many frustrations with our medical system and my insurance company. Why did I need a referral from my main physician to see a specialist obviously needed, before my insurance would pay for it? So dumb!

At my young age, I was not familiar with the word *colonoscopy*. The doctor described the procedure, and it made me feel sick... *yuck*. A scope up my butt while I was unconscious. He reassured me I wouldn't feel a thing. What he *didn't* tell me was that the prep day beforehand would be explosive. As the procedure drew near, my thoughts of what could happen while I was under sedation consumed me. This scared the crap out of me—literally!

What if I farted?

Would they find anything strange up there?

What if I shit all over the doctor?

The day before the colonoscopy, I couldn't eat anything, only clear liquids. I could have broth, Jello, Gatorade, and popsicles, but nothing colored red. For heaven's sakes, people with bowel issues shouldn't be having sugary, chemical-filled food before a procedure like this! {Get used to my rants; in this section, as they will be coming in hot.}

Once the noon hour came, I was instructed to take two stool softeners. My stools hadn't been solid in months. Later in the afternoon, I had to start drinking this gallon jug of GoLYTELY—no shit! I think the better brand name would be Colon Blow. Between the pills and this salty, chemical-filled liquid, I threw up in the kitchen while shitting my pants. Not that I was a stranger to that, but it was so uncontrollable and embarrassing to the nth degree.

Thankfully, Husband #1 had been in nursing school and was familiar with bodily fluids. I slept with a towel under my ass, but—pun intended—after what had occurred, there couldn't be anything left inside me.

The next day, we drove to the hospital, my butt cheeks clenched with another towel on the seat of the car. They hooked me up to an IV, and nighty night I went. When I woke from sedation, I felt as if they hadn't even touched me. Not sure which seemed scarier—the knowing or not knowing.

The doctor came into my room with the diagnosis: *Crohn's disease*. He explained a lot after that, but as I lay there, still drowsy from the drugs, all I could comprehend was the word *disease*. Then, tears began to swell in my eyes.

> *At first, she feels a strange sense of relief. There is a diagnosis for what she's experiencing, and maybe now she can get help, but that relief is short-lived. The realization that she will be labeled forever makes her feel alone in a world she knows nothing about.*

So many thoughts were zooming in my head as suddenly I was labeled with a disease.

- ♥ Could I get life insurance?
- ♥ What about side effects?
- ♥ Would I become dependent on medications?
- ♥ Was I going to die?
- ♥ Is there a cure?
- ♥ How would this affect my daily life?
- ♥ Would I be able to care for my kids?
- ♥ What the hell is Crohn's disease?

Since I knew *nothing* about Crohn's, I relied entirely on my doctor to educate me. He informed me that Crohn's disease is a chronic inflammatory condition that can affect any part of the digestive tract. Crohn's causes the immune system to mistakenly attack the healthy tissues of the digestive system, leading to abdominal pain, diarrhea, fatigue and fever, which I was very familiar with by this time.

The disease was prevalent in my terminal ileum, which is where the last part of the small intestine (ileum) joins the beginning of the large intestine (cecum). A valve there regulates the flow of fluids through the two, called the ileocecal junction. The function of the ileum is to absorb nutrients, especially B-12. Since it is an autoimmune condition, my immune system had been weakened. Basically, my body was fighting itself off in my bowels, like it would a virus. This explained why I had been so tired and felt like I had the flu so often, even with a fever.

I started to grasp how this disease had taken hold of my daily life.

One would think that exploring my eating habits would be a top priority. Yet, to my surprise, my doctor's focus was on medications, so I became another Big Pharma client. I reluctantly admit that prescription meds were a ray of sunshine, at first. I began to have less bloating, and bathroom visits were not as urgent as before.

My new three-part protocol consisted of Mesalamine, to reduce inflammation in the gastrointestinal tract, Methotrexate, which suppresses the immune system to control inflammation, and steroids, which are used during a flare up. The common objective of these medications: *reduce inflammation*.

The medications came with many challenges. Some helped for a while, but the side effects often made me feel worse than the disease itself. I quickly learned that steroids caused horrible side effects. Massive hunger, weight gain, sleepless nights, and uncontrolled irritability were not at all what I had anticipated or hoped for.

Then, to my surprise, these medications suddenly became ineffective. They literally stopped working. It was back to square one—another descent in the roller coaster ride. I had to attempt new medications and navigate a complex variety of treatment options. The ray of sunshine was gone, and I was in desperate need of a new approach.

I know that I didn't take my diagnosis as seriously as I should have: I was young and just wanted to live my life. Looking back, I can see that the flare-ups typically happened after a stressful life event or prior to a big vacation, since anticipation ramped things up in my gut.

Being full of energy my entire life, I could easily conceal my anxieties through constant movement or non-stop action. Multitasking was a facade to cover up my symptoms. I appeared to be in control from the outside, but on the inside, my body felt buzzed all day long. For years, I lived in a haze of exhaustion and frustration. Life was mere survived, living without enthusiasm, while the disease held control.

After doctor appointments and more testing there were new prescriptions. I was now stuck on a merry-go-round, and I couldn't get off.

The pills quit working, and eventually, I was put on Remicade.

Remicade is the brand name for a medication used to treat various inflammatory conditions, including Crohn's disease. It belongs to a class of drugs called biologics. Remicade works by targeting and blocking TNF, a protein that plays a role in inflammation. By reducing TNF levels, Remicade helps to control inflammation in the body and alleviate symptoms associated with conditions like Crohn's disease. It is administered through an IV and is typically given in a doctor's office or an infusion center under close supervision.

These drugs take nine months to develop, hence the cost to my insurance equated to approximately $4,000 for every infusion, which was administered every eight weeks. Thank goodness I had good insurance: my copay was only $100.

Taking time off work, explaining to everybody why, and being frustrated with the medical community was just the beginning.

Fortunately, Nurse Stephanie, who administered the IV drug, was a much-needed source of happiness in my life.

Due to the regularity of my visits, every eight weeks, and the two hours it took to administer the IV, we got to know each other. We chatted about life and our teenage daughters. The laughter and friendship served as medicine, too. Every infusion left me feeling bloated, exhausted, and drained for days.

I was both puzzled and intrigued by the fact that Stephanie regularly received complimentary lunches from the Remicade pharmaceutical rep. Basically, sales representatives offer food and various promotional items like pens and notepads to the staff, aiming to capture their attention and encourage doctors to prescribe the drug they represent, instead of their competitors'. Wouldn't they just prescribe what is best for the patient? It seems absurd that something as trivial as a large pepperoni pizza could influence the medication prescribed by your doctor. This angered me and fueled my desire to learn more about my medications. I wanted to understand their impact on my body, as well as the potential side effects.

I learned that Remicade can lead to the development of other autoimmune disorders. This can cause the immune system to mistakenly attack healthy tissues in the body, potentially leading to conditions like lupus, multiple sclerosis, or autoimmune hepatitis. Some of the other possible side effects included: risks of other infections, allergic reactions (that is why I was given Benadryl before the IV), possible heart failure, and increased risk of certain cancers such as lymphoma or skin cancer. WTF!

Can you imagine paying thousands of dollars a month for your medication, only to realize it could possibly cause more damage than good? It was time to take control of my health!

Deep down, she refuses to accept that this will be her fate. There has to be another way. She feels trapped and tethered to Big Pharma. The longer she stays in the system, the more she realizes this isn't healing—it just manages symptoms and does not address the root cause. Her questions fuel her desire to research more about this disease.

"I have Crohn's disease; Crohn's disease doesn't have me."
—Andrew (Andy) Mac Isaac

Diverting without Doctors

I started exploring a range of remedies and natural approaches to wellness. This was not a quick-fix solution like I would have preferred. It became a slow, often painful process of trial and error, learning to listen to my body and trust my intuition.

Making small changes to my diet first, I eliminated foods that triggered symptoms and focused on nourishing my body with whole, natural ingredients. At one point, I drank aloe vera juice to calm the inflammation. Of course, I didn't stick with it long enough to see any changes.

At this time, I owned my coffee shop and had started networking to grow my customer base. On one very memorable day, at the local Chamber of Commerce, as I exchanged business cards with another member, my attention diverted to two unfamiliar faces walking in. These two tall blondes were not only beautifully dressed and put together, but they were twins. They radiated with a glow that oozed *healthy*. I had no idea why they were there, but I wanted whatever they had or were selling.

After chatting with them for a bit, we swapped cards and said our goodbyes. When I got home, I rushed to my computer and looked up their website: The Raw Body Twins Coaching, designed to help women navigate the raw vegan world. I grew intrigued. Connecting the dots didn't take long. Their glow was directly related to the food they ate, and their beautiful bodies were shaped by working out at home. They were the model of health that I desperately wanted and needed!

Their program was not cheap, so I sold some old patio furniture to afford it. It's funny how we learn some of these tactics in childhood but don't think about until later in life. Like back in the Money Monster chapter, how my mom had garage sales so we could afford a night out.

These twins were my first glimpse of hope to help me manage my disease holistically. I became a model student for their program, and I followed everything they said to a T. This was when I started my raw vegan diet. But I also began to address the emotional toll of living with a chronic illness.

Stress and anxiety had become my constant companions, so I began to do the home workouts they suggested, which helped tremendously. The symptoms that had once ruled my life started to fade. The bathroom trips became less frequent. The cramping and urgency that had dictated my days loosened their grip. For the first time in years, I felt like I was finally living—not just surviving. The bonus to all of this was, I lost weight and felt less inflamed.

Without permission from anyone, this girl exited the medical system. I called and cancelled my upcoming infusion, saying to myself, "Screw this shit, I'm done!" For six glorious years, I lived happy and healthy. I felt strong, vibrant, and free of the symptoms that had plagued me for a decade.

My journey to reclaiming my health felt complete, and I wore that victory like a badge of honor. I continued doing my home workouts thru Beachbody, plus I began online fitness coaching and fell in love with helping clients take control of their health, like I thought I had. Then the unthinkable happened.

Name of the Beast

It crept in slowly. So subtly, I could easily pretend it wasn't happening. A bit of bloating after a meal and some fatigue, I chalked up to being stressed and busy—nothing I couldn't handle. But I couldn't take any more chances. My persistence around finding a holistic approach led me to a functional medicine doctor.

I liked that this practitioner would treat the whole body and get to the root of my problem, instead of just writing a scrip for some side-effect-laden pill. I began taking herbal supplements, things such as Ashwagandha, Boswellia, and Slippery Elm. He also ordered a food intolerance test.

At this point, I had already cut out gluten, dairy, corn, and soy from my diet, so I became excited to discover what else could be wrecking my insides and causing the return of symptoms. I started to go to the new doctor's office a few times a week for adjustments as I awaited my results.

Pills never were and still are not my favorite things to take. It's not that I am unable to swallow them; it's more about my resistance to having a pill box, after seeing my grandma's box full of prescriptions medications.

To the doctor's surprise and mine, there were no foods in the highly intolerant category, but there was a long list of medium-range food sensitivities. I began to omit everything on that list, even the spices. I committed to his program, and it helped—for a bit. Gradually, my confident strut into the holistic appointments changed back into slow walks as I hunched over in abdominal pain.

My symptoms didn't ease up; in fact, they multiplied, each one bigger than the last. It felt like someone who had turned off a light in my bright life and made everything dark again. My once-flat, toned stomach began to swell, becoming tight and distended, as though I was six months pregnant, once again. The discomfort became unrelenting. Every meal was a gamble, every bite threatening to ignite a storm of cramping and bloating. My clothes no longer fit, and I dreaded the thought of wearing a swimsuit.

I followed the rules. I ate clean, worked out regularly, and avoided anything that might harm my body. Yet here I was, feeling worse than ever. I began to question everything I thought I knew.

Was I wrong?

Did my dedication to holistic health and fitness somehow backfire?

Had I done irreparable damage to my body by turning away from conventional medicine years earlier?

How could I preach the gospel of health and wellness to others when my own body betrayed me?

Shame washed over me in waves. I coached others on how to take control of their health, yet I couldn't control my own. The very foundation of my identity felt like it was crumbling beneath me. I started to plummet, consumed by the overwhelming feeling that I was nothing more than a fraud.

> *That's when she meets him: the Gut Monster. She doesn't name him right away. At first, she doesn't even acknowledge him. Denial becomes her closest ally, whispering sweet nothings that this will all just be temporary. "You're fine," it says. "This will pass."*
>
> *This Monster has been lurking inside for years, festering and biding his time, waiting for the perfect moment to attack. And now, with fiery breath and bulging, menacing eyes, it is ready to wage war against her. He doesn't just attack her body; he goes after her mind and spirit, too. Denial protects her from the reality of what can happen, but it isn't enough to keep his attacks at bay.*
>
> *Depression, a companion she never thought she would meet, quietly joins the chaos. She doesn't say the word "depression" out loud for a long time. It feels foreign, impossible, like it doesn't belong in her world. Depression happens to other people—those who didn't have her drive, energy, or resilience. But there it is, creeping in, making itself at home.*
>
> *It whispers, "You're failing," "You'll never get better," "Why even try?" The ruminating thoughts need an answer. The only thing that comes to her: "You are strong and can handle it." There has to be a lesson amidst this battle.*

The morning shifts I worked at my coffee shop became a struggle when that turned out to be the time of day when I was in the worst pain. Customers asked if I felt okay as I doubled over at the cash register.

The realization that I might possibly need to sell my franchise came as another punch to the face. Owning a business was stressful enough, and something had to give… So, that is what did. I sold my coffee shop. But I felt like a failure, and that fueled my anxiety, which became exponentially worse, just like my pain did.

> "The road to health is paved with good *intestine*!"
> —Sherry A. Rodgers

Jumping Back on the Ride

Mark and I were on the verge of making one of our dreams come true in the next year: retiring and moving to the lake full time. I had envisioned lazy afternoons by the water, long walks in nature, and a peaceful, non-city life, but that began to feel out of reach. It was a vision I could no longer see. The timing of all of this really sucked. Not as if getting sick is ever a good time, but dammit!

Desperation led me back into the world of medicine—a place I had sworn off years before. The condescending looks from the doctors said it all: "This is what happens when you stop the treatment. You brought this on yourself." I f***ing hated them all!

Every appointment felt like a defeat, every prescription like a slap in the face. I cycled through medications, each one promising relief but I got no results. I found myself in and out of emergency rooms, pumped full of steroids and then discharged quickly, since I felt so healthy otherwise. No medication seemed to work, and my doctor didn't seem interested in doing more tests, so I left to find a new G.I.

I had stuck with the same doctor who had diagnosed me in 1996, but honestly, I never did like him. In prior years, when I brought up conversations around food and how it was affecting me, he had always shooed me off that topic. He saw no nutritional connection to Crohn's, and prescribing drugs seemed to be his only method of treatment. I needed a physician who would take a different approach, who would listen to me and work with me, not against me.

Every meal felt like a landmine. Foods I had once considered safe turned against me, leaving me bloated, cramping, and in the fetal position. I took pride in my fitness, but now my reflection in the mirror showed a stranger—a woman with a distended belly, sunken eyes, and hollow cheeks. Death describes it best. I deteriorated, not just on the inside but now my symptoms were visible on the outside. I had hidden it well until now.

I knew there had to be more to what was going on in my body beyond just inflammation. After being hospitalized for the second time in the same month, doctors ordered a CT scan. My veins were now shrinking, so starting an IV became the latest frustration.

I had to drink a special prep for this procedure, too, and it brought about more tears. I almost vomited multiple times—and I am not a puker.

When the results were in, they revealed I had significant inflammation and some blockages. It became apparent it was time for me to spend a few days in the hospital, where I would be pumped full of more steroids and who knows what else.

The G.I. doctor who happened to be on call, when I was admitted, is the one I chose to work with, going forward. He was younger and seemed very knowledgeable and willing to get to the bottom of this. During my hospital stays, the nurses often commented on how healthy I seemed, because I would not stay in my bed, like most patients.

I walked the halls nonstop. I knew that movement was important for recovery and lying in bed did no good. In CNA school, I'd learned that blood clots, bed sores, and sorrow could be mine, if I didn't get up and move. Lord knows, I didn't need anything else to make me more depressed.

The nurses and I had conversations about how horrible the hospital slop they served was for the patients. It featured ingredients like sugar, corn syrup, and other inflammatory crap. Thankfully, Mark brought me healthy smoothies or his homemade broth. Even the broth at the hospital turned out to be ladened with bad additives. This frustrated me to no end.

On this go-round, I didn't mind the little weight gain I put on, due to the steroids flowing into my veins during my hospital stay, as it filled in my hollow cheeks.

> *Her spirit diminishes. The once-strong woman is now feeble. She sinks so deep into a state of depression; denial becomes the only thing protecting her from giving up hope. Her family grows frustrated, as they can see what she cannot—the truth about her disease.*

Over the months, as I tried to get more answers, the high-dosage steroids were helping some of my symptoms, but the side effects were brutal. My mood swings, combined with a lack of sleep, compromised my mental state. Every time I attempted to taper off the steroids, my Gut Monster reared its ugly head, which led me back to the little white pills. My body was becoming addicted to steroids.

I started trying other medications, such as the new-to-market biologics, but nothing worked. Time started to become a critical factor. I only weighed 110 pounds now and I was losing weight rapidly.

> *Surgery is her biggest fear, but realistically, she knows maybe it is on the horizon. Denial is being swallowed up by the Gut Monster, too, forcing her to face reality.*

The 2017 holiday season came and went. I spent most of my time indoors, in my pajamas, sleeping, when I could, in the fetal position. It felt like Groundhog Day. I would go to bed about 10:00 p.m. My bowels would wake up about 11:00 p.m. Then the cycle started: pain pills, hot baths, rocking on all fours, cringing, more pain pills, and wanting to talk to somebody so bad.

Mark had to sleep, since he had to get up at 4:30 a.m. There was no reason for both of us to be exhausted. But being in excruciating pain in the middle of the night, with no remedy, is scary—like you're in hell. On a scale of one to ten, which is something I answered often at the hospital, my pain was at a thousand.

If I was lucky, I could get to sleep around 6:00 a.m., but by 10:00 a.m., I woke up when the hydrocodone wore off, and, once again, I was in horrible pain. On many mornings, my mom came over to comfort me with a back rub and a heating pad. I am sure it became a hell for her, too, watching me cry and return to the fetal position.

Mark felt so guilty, but he had taken so much time off already and his retirement was soon. If it hadn't been for my family and friends, this battle would have been lost. I would have given up. To comfort me during the day, I would visit a few of my Crohn's disease groups on Facebook. I didn't have the energy to verbally talk to anybody or engage in much conversation, but it was comforting when I was in that online space.

I had given up my coaching, since supporting others took too much of what I didn't have—energy and self-confidence. Mark and I agreed that I would probably never work again, but we could figure that out later. That is how desolate my life started to look.

> "Pain is inevitable, but misery is optional."
> —Tim Hansel

Now I Know my CBDs

During my quest to find pain relief, I had several friends suggest using marijuana. I had smoked pot in high school, but in no way was weed a part of our lives. But I refused to give up. As my exploration for natural pain remedies broadened, I began to see more and more information about CBD.

I had heard good things about this plant medicine from a friend, who used it for his dog's arthritis with success. Stella, my boxer, suffered from knee pain, as well. I figured, why not find some CBD we both could take? Can't hurt, right?

I started my research and quickly learned that CBD was good for pain, getting quality sleep and reducing inflammation, and for a list of other symptoms. I needed all those things, and, even though it's a member of the cannabis family, it was legal.

Amazon was my source for shopping, since I wasn't leaving the house much. After my fair share of scrolling and reading product descriptions, I landed on a great deal. A full pint for only $30. Could this be the miracle I was looking for, and could it really be so cheap and readily available? Was it there all along, and I just didn't know about it?

My excitement outweighed any sense of frustration as I anxiously awaited another possible solution for my pain. As I think back to that pivotal day, I can't help but chuckle at the sight of what I had hoped would be my magic elixir. It was nothing more than an oversized bottle filled with a thin, green, watery substance.

That very same day, a member of the Crohn's disease Facebook group I popped into regularly, posted about their positive experiences with CBD. They expressed how it had significantly alleviated their symptoms and brought them much-needed relief. Their post piqued my curiosity. As I dove deeper into researching this brand, it became very apparent that the product I had ordered from Amazon was *not* CBD, and was more of a hoax.

Filled with hope and anticipation again, I swiftly clicked the "Order Now" button, eager to receive a bottle of legit CBD and see if it would deliver the same benefits as testified to by others. This was no Amazon, and shipping took forever, but immediately after my first delivery of CBD arrived, I began microdosing twice a day. After just two days of my new protocol, I was sleeping better, which, in turn, led to more energy. I felt more relaxed, and my pain slightly decreased.

I vividly recall the moment when, overcome with emotion, I went live on social media. Tears were streaming down my face as I shared about the new product I had discovered. It was a significant milestone for me, because, after a prolonged period of confinement, I had the courage and strength to leave the house. I even took the extra step of applying makeup, wanting to embrace this newfound hope. I could sense my wings were starting to grow back!

That tiny one-ounce bottle of CBD proved to be a powerhouse, a catalyst for change that delivered an immense feeling of empowerment after I had suffered so much. It was as if someone had opened a door, allowing rays of sunshine to filter through. Those rays were exactly what I needed to gather the strength to persevere and continue my fight, because it wasn't over yet.

After a month of microdosing, I was able to slowly reduce my dosage of hydrocodone, and my sleep significantly approved. A strong conviction started to grow within me that I could make a meaningful difference in the lives of others! Motivated by this newfound passion, I took a leap and partnered with this CBD company, determined to spread the word about its potential benefits. I couldn't bear keeping this extraordinary discovery to myself; I had to share it with the world.

Prior to my falling ill, my business revolved primarily around physical fitness and specific dietary approaches, both of which were no longer feasible for me. However, sharing my personal journey of managing my Crohn's with CBD and how it had instilled hope in my life became second nature.

Despite the positive impact CBD had on my well-being, my battle was far from over, and the possibility of undergoing surgery still loomed ahead of me. Warriors, prepare for battle once again!

She smiles, something she hasn't done in a long time. Her mind and body need a boost. Is this just a placebo effect? Or are the results she's experiencing truly real? She doesn't care, since this acts as the life raft, she needs to save herself from drowning.

During my second month on this protocol, I managed to taper off my steroids with no major flare ups—this seemed *huge*! And there was more good news: I was nearly off my pain pills and finally sleeping like a baby.

Even though I felt less pain as more time passed, I had trouble digesting solid food. Mashed potatoes, broth, soup, and smoothies were all I could eat without puking. Nothing seemed to stay down. This became a new concern. In March, my G.I. doctor ordered an MRI. After being called back for the procedure, I found myself in a very cold room, drinking a horrible Sprite-like concoction. It took five sticks before they could find a vein to start the IV.

She is alone with the tears. Bruising arms, exhaustion, and nauseated from the prep—she honestly just wants to die. Wasting away to nothing sounds like the best answer for her.

I was instructed to lie on my cramping stomach. Tears saturated the pillow my head rested on. The repeated beeping from the machine only made things worse. No one could hear my sobbing from inside this long, hollow tube.

Then, they injected me with a contrast in my ass that burned like the hell I was in. It came from all directions like a freight train that had lost its brakes. I can honestly say it ranks as one of the top-ten worst days of my life.

Then, I had to wait for the results.

Excuse Me, WTF Did You Say?

Unfortunately, my follow-up appointment was scheduled for a time when my husband couldn't be with me, due to the demands of his work and upcoming retirement.

When my GI doctor came into the exam room, his expression alone told me that something was seriously wrong. He began to explain that my bowels were twisted and entangled like a coiled garden hose, and I had developed fistulas, abnormal tunnels connecting one part of my bowel to another. Suddenly, as he unraveled the reality of my internal turmoil, my tangled gut, the excruciating pain I had experienced started to make sense!

But the most unexpected blow came when he said, based on the MRI results, there was a possibility of malignant cancer in my sigmoid colon. I was taken aback, unable to comprehend the gravity of his words. I couldn't even summon tears; I was drained, shocked, and numb.

Finally, the doctor handed me a card with the name and phone number for a colorectal surgeon, stressing that time was of the essence.

I had to wait for Mark to pick me up from my mother's later that day, but his reaction to hearing my news—the look on his face, the paleness of his complexion, and the silence—conveyed volumes. He struggled to find the right words, plus he was consumed by guilt for not being there when I received my devastating news. I knew he felt useless, wishing he could do more for me.

Honestly, I felt so bad for him. Mark was due to retire soon, and then, we were going to sell our home and embark on our dream of moving to the lake. Even as my gut put a damper on all of this, Mark was the last person to complain about it. I am thankful every day that our stars aligned!

Fortunately, when I called the surgeon's office, they were able to schedule my consultation for the following Monday due to a cancelation.

> *All she can think about is who she will be leaving behind: her wonderful husband, her daughters, other family, and friends. She has fought this battle so hard, but to no avail. Defeated once again. The Gut Monster arrives to deliver the final blow. Her entire spirit begins to give up as the word cancer consumes her.*

That weekend felt like an eternity. I was full of fear and uncertainty about the impending bowel resection. It was a daunting, exhausting, and emotionally draining two days. I tried my best not to dwell on the dreadful possibilities associated with cancer, but when one is already battling depression, fatigue, and malnourishment, finding a glimmer of positivity becomes increasingly challenging.

I visited the colorectal surgeon and, with tearful eyes, handed her the envelope with my results. She offered some reassurance right away, stating she believed the mass was an abscess rather than cancer, but surgery was still necessary and had to be performed promptly. She also informed me I would require a temporary or possibly permanent ostomy bag, depending on the outcome. That news hit me like a powerful blast, once again leaving me in a state of shock.

Before the consultation wrapped up, I informed the surgeon about my CBD usage and how I had tapered off steroids. To my relief, she expressed support for continuing with the CBD oil until the day of surgery, emphasizing that, by eliminating steroids, I could anticipate a smoother recovery. She clarified that extended steroid usage can suppress the adrenal glands, which in turn can result in complications during and after surgery. This occurs because the body may struggle to adequately respond to the stress induced by a surgical procedure.

Surgery was scheduled, and I followed doctors' orders diligently, while continuing my CBD regime.

> *She feels relieved that this all will be over soon. She can relax, hoping, as cancer becomes a word of the past, she will get the spark she needs to deal with her other news—the bag.*

While I waited for surgery day, April 18, to arrive, I reached a point of acceptance. I was able to acknowledge the potential reality of living with an ostomy bag and the prospect of managing it for the rest of my life. Ostomy bags save lives, but they come with a huge inconvenience.

- ♥ Could I swim in the lake?
- ♥ What if it leaked?
- ♥ What about the smell?
- ♥ Could I still have sex?

So many embarrassing situations ran through my mind. It would be a significant adjustment—one I never imagined I would have to face.

Bye-Bye Bowels

I was filled with a mix of excitement and dread as the day approached. Once I checked into my pre-op room, I took funny pictures, hoping to look back someday and laugh.

They used markers to make a circle on my belly where the bag would be attached. As I was prepped to be sedated, I bid farewell to my mom and husband, and then the nurses wheeled me down the hospital corridor. It was time to conquer this beast!

Surgery lasted a grueling five hours. As I slowly emerged from the depths of anesthesia, my first instinct was to feel my abdomen. Of course, I couldn't feel anything yet, as I was barely regaining consciousness, but I anxiously searched for any sign of the dreaded ostomy bag. Just maybe it was there, concealed beneath bandages.

When the nurse entered the room, I anxiously asked, "Where's my ostomy bag?"

A smile graced her face as she responded, "Turns out you didn't need one."

Those words brought a tidal wave of relief, and I burst into tears.

I was overcome with gratitude, though still confused by the sedation and the unexpected news. I was wheeled back to my room, where I was reunited with my family. Together, we celebrated. There were tears of joy and relief at the news of no ostomy bag.

When the surgeon later visited, the news continued to improve. No cancer! They had successfully removed twelve inches from my small intestine and eighteen inches from my sigmoid colon, where the suspected cancer was dwelling. During the pre-surgery consultation, I was told to anticipate a minimum of seven days in the hospital, with the possibility of an extended stay depending on the circumstances. However, to my surprise, I was discharged after only three days.

During my short hospital stay, I made sure I doubled up on my CBD protocol, to assist in recovery. Two weeks later, at my post-surgery appointment, I amazed the nurses by being able to walk upright as they guided me down the hallway to the examination room. The surgeon entered with a mix of astonishment and delight, proclaiming my recovery to be nothing short of a miracle, as most people who undergo that type of surgery do not bounce back that fast.

The following week, I had a follow-up appointment with my GI doctor, and he, too, was stunned by the success of the procedure and the positive outcome. In October 2018, I scheduled a colonoscopy, and to my immense relief, there was no evidence of any disease! With the aid of CBD and my persistence, victory against the Gut Monster was mine! I made a firm decision never to see that doctor again!

Her mental state improves by the minute. She is so happy but still has reservations, as only time will tell whether that Monster has left for good. She smiles as she types this. :)

Beyond the Battle

During my recovery period, I reflected on the many wars within—not just with my gut, but with my mind. I have always been a high-energy person who took pride in managing multiple tasks simultaneously. The sensation I had inside that I *thought* was energy was anxiety. That is when I began to connect the dots between the brain and my gut.

Over the decades, as I approached a big event or anticipated an upcoming vacation, I would suddenly find myself in one of my Crohn's flare-ups—bloated and feeling yucky, as I described in earlier parts of this chapter. The anxiety I was experiencing was affecting my disease. How I didn't see the connection before was mind-blowing!

As I read during my Holistic Wellness Coaching Academy Course, anxiety and stress can significantly impact Crohn's disease in several ways:

- Aggravating Symptoms: It can exacerbate the symptoms of Crohn's disease and flare-ups may become more frequent, leading to increased discomfort and pain.

- Gut-Brain Connection: The gut and brain are interconnected through the gut-brain axis. This is called the vagus nerve. Anxiety and stress can disrupt this communication, leading to changes in gut motility, sensitivity, and secretion, which can worsen Crohn's symptoms.

- Immune Response: It can weaken the immune system, making it more difficult for the body to control inflammation associated with Crohn's Disease.

I continued to take my CBD oil. In January after my surgery, eight months later, I discovered the power of this plant once again.

One morning, during a vacation in Mexico, I squeezed the dropperful of CBD into my mouth and then proceeded to knock over the bottle. The whole contents spilled. Shit, what a mess! I cleaned it up and didn't think much about the fact that I wouldn't have it to take over the remaining vacation time.

A few days later, I was going to a scheduled massage when, as I was running up the stairs to the spa, I felt like my chest had hit a brick wall. This was a familiar sensation but something I couldn't pinpoint.

My first thought was chest pains, but as I lay there on the massage table, trying to relax, it dawned on me. It was anxiety—another dot connected! The CBD had obviously been doing more than I'd originally thought. Now, after being without it for a few days, my body was revolting.

Unfortunately, I had not brought a backup bottle of oil, so I spent the entire rest of the trip in a state of unrest. The turbulent, delayed flight home added even more stress and anxiety. Once I was home, I religiously took my oil and slowly began to feel like myself again. To this day, I have not experienced an episode like that again. The power of this plant saved me in many ways!

In beginning, I often asked, 'Why me?' I struggled with the unfairness of it all, questioning why my body had turned against me. But over time, that question began to shift. I started to ask, 'Why not me?' What made me any different from anyone else facing hardship? That shift didn't take away the pain or uncertainty, but it gave me a new sense of purpose and resilience. This disease may have chosen me, but I've chosen how to live with it—with strength, acceptance, and the hope that sharing my story might help someone else on their own roller coaster ride.

Today, in February 2025, almost seven years later, I can proudly say I am free from this monster and the medical merry-go-round. I take no prescription medications and have not seen a G.I. doctor since that last colonoscopy. This transformation has become my life's mission.

As a Wellness Consultant, I've had the privilege of helping others reduce their reliance on medications and discover the freedom that comes with taking control of their health. I've seen firsthand how empowering it can be.

You don't have to settle for survival.

You don't have to accept a life dictated by illness.

There is hope, and there is a way forward.

I'm living proof of that.

FINDING HER

SECTION 2
HER ALLIES

"The strongest people are not those who show strength in front of the world but those who fight and win battles that others do not know anything about."
—Jonathan Harnisch, *The Brutal Truth*

FINDING HER

Ally 1

Mom

She showed me resilience, the ability to bounce back in the face of challenges, losses, and adversity.

THE CONNECTION BETWEEN my mom and I began when I grew in the womb, like for most of us. But our beginning was a little different, as I described much earlier. What I didn't tell you is I was born on my mom's eighteenth birthday. Surprise! Oh, what a joyous celebration for her... eye roll!

She tells me stories about my long nails and body hair. For some reason, I didn't cook long enough. She passed her due date by two weeks, but I only weighed in at four pounds, ten ounces. Her strength during this challenging time was what I needed to journey through life. She planted that seed early!

My mom worked very hard, and her skills with numbers helped us stay afloat as she navigated being single. She enrolled in college and worked way beyond forty hours a week, plus was attending classes at night. I never recall her being weak or feeble, just being strong and a force I became scared to reckon with.

Her strength in accounting school landed her a good career as the CFO of an engineering firm. The skirt ensemble she wore, with heels and hose, resembled her personality — professional and confident. One thing she often told me and my brother: "Life isn't fair, and if you think it's so much better at someone else's house, then go live there." She meant it, and we knew it.

As I transitioned into life as a teenager, she and I started butting heads. Mostly, the typical teenager stuff, like sneaking out, drinking, and eventually having sex. I resented her for the strict rules and the constant punishments and grounding me during this time.

After she divorced, she only dated one time, since her busy career and children kept her focused. My mom proved to be a great role model. She tried to teach me that being single would not be a bad thing. I'm sure she hoped I would follow in her footsteps.

Instead, I rebelled, and that's when I started being promiscuous. The first time I snuck out, I got caught. She was no dummy! When I woke up in my boyfriend's arms, I realized the clock showed 6:00 a.m.

"Holy shit! I am in so much trouble," I thought. I didn't live far from him, but it seemed like miles away, as I ran home, trying to wrap my head around what I would say. I had snuck out the back sliding-glass door the night before, after she fell asleep.

When I arrived home, the front door looked open. I knew the shit was about to hit the fan! The look on her face as she asked me where I had been all night stabbed a knife into me.

My brain responded stupidly, "I took a jog around the block." She knew I was lying. After I spilled the beans, her look of disappointment was one I would see many times in my life. I hated that look, that made tears well up in my eyes.

After some discussion, she agreed to take me to my first gynecological appointment, hoping to go home with a prescription for birth control. I was relieved but also so shameful, after that morning's event. I felt like a slut.

Looking back, I am so thankful for her persistent punishment. Even though she tried to teach me about "not needing a man," it was without much success.

She started dating a man when I was in high school, and they married when I turned seventeen. He is still my stepdad, and I love him dearly. They built a house, and we all lived together for about a year, before I moved out on my own. That is probably why we all still like each other.

Her support during my first marriage proved amazing. Our relationship grew very close when I found myself alone during the first pregnancy due to his deployment overseas.

Even though Hubby One was there for my second pregnancy, she still supported me by coming over and timing my false contractions while he worked. They seemed to go on for weeks!

My parents were spectacular grandparents for my girls. I am thankful my kids had these wonderful role models during a time in my life when I may have not been one.

I looked to my mom for advice on many things, even though I knew I wouldn't like what she had to stay. She taught me about listing the pros and cons, when purchasing something large, a lesson I still use. You make that list, and then your answer will appear clearer. She was the expert at taking emotions out of things and checking off the boxes, when it came to getting things done.

My mom worked as a CFO at the same company for twenty years. She lived in the same house for thirty-three years and has been with my stepdad for thirty-eight years. Even though I embrace change, which she does not love, I have learned that consistency in daily life does pay off.

The resilience she instilled in me has helped me fight many battles of life. She is the ally who taught me to be a warrior.

> "A warrior is not born; they are forged in the fires of a mother's tough love."
> —Author Unknown

… ANGIE LICKLITER

ALLY 2

GRANDPARENTS

*They granted me unconditional love,
love without judgment or expectations.*

MY GRANDPARENTS, Norman and Della, were the rock of our family and my heroes. Since my mom was an unwed mother, my grandparents helped take care of me until my mom got married, when I was seven months old. The bond that formed between us had a lasting impact on me.

My grandpa worked in construction, and grandma was a homemaker. She never worked outside of the home, but that doesn't mean she wasn't busy. In addition to raising four kids, they owned rental properties she helped maintain. My grandma also baked, canned, cared for their garden and flowers, sang in the choir, and loved to play golf.

Norman was a stern man and grew up in a house of twelve brothers and sisters during the Great Depression. He worked very hard to support his family, leaving home before the sun came up and returning just in time for dinner.

Sundays were his days off, and I love my memories of him chasing us around their expansive ranch home, playing tag. After the chase, the rest of the morning was dedicated to the Lutheran Church, to which they were very devoted and tithed weekly.

Della also had twelve brothers and sisters, and she was a twin. For as long as I can remember, she struggled with her weight, and her large breasts didn't help. I considered myself blessed to have those, as well. Jenny Craig, the Diet Center, and Weight Watchers are a few of the programs I remember her trying. She often sang at weddings, and that always motivated her to start another diet. Her voice sounded beautiful. I can hear her singing now, as she looks down from heaven.

After we moved from Washington to Kansas, my grandparents flew out for Thanksgiving or Christmas each year. The airport goodbyes left me in tears every time. Once my mom was single, she needed help, so they flew my brother and I back to Washington for extended stays over the summer. They spoiled us with shopping excursions for new clothes and school supplies to take back home.

My memories of those summers still flood my eyes with happiness. Denny's on Friday night, for example. My grandparents loved their clam chowder, and we were allowed to have breakfast food for dinner, which was a treat.

The Golden Steer was a family favorite for diner classics. My cousins and I loved their treasure box, filled with stickers, plastic watches, tattoos, and bracelets for the good kids who finished their meal.

When my male cousins visited from Alaska, I turned into a tomboy and enjoyed playing in the dirt and riding the tractor. I loved leaving behind the worries of who I was back home in Kansas.

Picking strawberries and raspberries with my grandma gave us time to talk. The actual picking of the berries was not fun and was tedious work, but I knew they needed to be picked. I always felt bad for my grandma, who did all the work to make those wonderful jams. The time I spent with her made every thorn worth it.

Behind their very long ranch home were greenhouses, tractors, pickup trucks, beautiful, landscaped grasses, and rows of apple trees. The garage roof was adjacent to the pool, so the brave among us used to jump from it. I never did, but many of my cousins and uncles took the plunge. Every time they did, I would worry my grandma might have a heart attack—she hated it!

My grandpa would just laugh as she screamed, *"Norman, don't let them jump off the roof!"*

Golf balls were little treasures we found around their property, because they liked to practice in their yard. We also enjoyed reading the *National Geographic* magazines, which were stacked miles high in the corner of their living room.

My grandparents were slow to accept technology, but finally, they got a satellite dish. It looked like a UFO in their driveway. My cousins and I could flip through the channels and suddenly be watching porn. This became a family joke, how Grandpa was watching the "fur" channel. He had no idea what we were talking about but just laughed along.

The wall of their garage was lined with canned foods and freezers, beside my grandma's Lincoln Town Car, which looked like a boat. The other garages housed a shop for the pool equipment and a place for my grandpa to tinker with things. There was also a garage with a ping-pong table and a separate guesthouse with a pool table.

I had two older female cousins who lived in Washington, and growing up, we were close. They became the summer sisters I'd never had. This changed once they entered their teens, and I became an annoying younger cousin.

Norman and Della's pool was a gathering place for friends and family. Daily visitors stopped by to lie beside the pool and enjoy their hospitality, which included sandwiches, lemonade, plus Grandma's homemade cookies and apple pies-a crowd favorite. My grandparents spent hours watering their beautiful hanging baskets and the gorgeous rhododendrons that surrounded their house. They won many awards for their Christmas décor, too, which included a manger scene, carolers, and a huge lit pine tree. Grandpa fell several times, trying to string lights, and even broke some bones. But he continued to decorate, year after year.

As they aged, my grandpa began to get dementia, so my grandparents had to move into assisted living. Sadly, they had to put him on a different floor in their community. After losing his independence, he died within a year of that move, when he was ninety-two years old.

Once my mom had retired, she decided to move grandma to Kansas, so we could spend time with her and help with the mounting doctor appointments. Grandma Della was now only fifteen minutes away from me, which made me very happy! We often played cards, went to lunch at her cafeteria, and took in Bingo on Thursday nights. Her love of rummy is something our whole family still enjoys.

My girls loved having her close, as they had a bond with her, like I did.

She always had profound advice, so when I asked her opinion on whether I should purchase the coffee shop, she replied, "If you don't do it, you will never know. If you do and fail, you will at least know." This nugget will stick with me forever!

My grandma took many medications, and my mom had the tedious task of filling her pill box weekly; keeping track of what medicine goes in each section is a nightmare for a anyone, let alone someone in their nineties. My love for health and wellness started to view these pills in a different light, and I grew frustrated at our medical system. How did they even know what worked?

When Grandma Della grew nearer to dying, some extended family flew in to spend some time with her and say their goodbyes. Thankfully, on her deathbed, her mind was still sharp, but her body began to shut down. This was quite different from her twin sister, who suffered from dementia while her body still thrived.

My mom and I spent a week at the nursing home, taking turns to grab a shower at home or eat a quick bite. Even though someone sat with her 24/7, I hated to leave Grandma Della even for a moment. I wanted to cherish every minute I could.

The night my mom decided to stay in the guest suite, down the hall, was when my grandma took her last breath. I was sleeping on the couch and awoke to the angels taking her. Grandma departed this Earth just as she should, in peace, at ninety-four years old. I feel so blessed to have been there during this time, as she had always been there for me.

FINDING HER

She died at 1:11 a.m. In numerology, 111 is often interpreted as an "angel number," signifying new beginnings, fresh starts, and positive potential. It encourages you to embrace new opportunities and trust your intuition as you move forward with confidence in your life. She is with God and looking down on me now. I feel her presence often.

I now love myself and others unconditionally, as my grandparents did.

> "The attitude of neutrality allows grandparents to listen to the teenager without the emotional baggage their parents carry. And if we listen carefully, we may be able to glimpse what the teenager is going through."
>
> —Jane Isay, *Unconditional Love: A Guide to Navigating the Joys and Challenges of Being a Grandparent Today*

ALLY 3

DAUGHTERS

*They delivered me strength
and became a source of motivation to keep going.*

MY FIRST DAUGHTER didn't want to come into the world when I wanted her to. Her dad was deployed, and she wanted him there at her birth. I, on the other hand, needed her out; she was what I held onto during some of the hardest months of my life. After twenty-four hours of labor and pushing for three more, I delivered a healthy baby girl.

Megan came into this world with a conehead full of black hair. Her chubby cheeks and skin tone resembled her father's. She was beautiful! Then, two years later, I found myself expecting again! Megan was very happy to have a sibling, and I felt thrilled to have another girl, since I had always wanted a sister, a friend for life.

With my second pregnancy, I had false contractions for what seemed to be an eternity, until my doctor finally agreed to induce my labor, two weeks after my due date. The doctor induced me at 8 a.m., and I bet him she would arrive before noon. That probably was wishful thinking on my part, but Lauren came into this world at noon, on the dot.

She was so pretty! No cone-shaped head, like her sister, fair skin like mine, but bald as an eagle. I consider myself lucky, as they were both good babies, and having two of them seemed easier.

My heart broke for them, when I decided to divorce their dad, but I did it for them. I couldn't let them see us like that anymore.

As they became teenagers, they developed very different personalities.

Megan made sure that everything and everyone appeared fine. Just like me, she didn't like to make waves, and she did everything she could to calm them. She often took over the role of a parent, when I battled with my monsters. Megan has a master's degree and is a high school social worker. I see her helping others just like she helped me. Her wonderful husband and two kids live close to us, and we love spending time with them.

Lauren was a little version of myself. The one to challenge me, as I challenged my mother. She was born with a strong desire to find her own identity and always pushed boundaries. Her resilience became an inherited gift. I gave her negative attention, though, while I fought my own war. Lauren is now a corrections officer and owns her own cleaning business. She hopes to become a detective in the future. I respect her drive and appreciate the reflections into my own life, as she is a lot like me. She is a single mom with a daughter, and sadly, we don't get to see them often, as they live in Kentucky.

I feel great sorrow for what my daughters endured during my struggles. But I know there is no going back and changing the past, therefore, I will go forth and join their battles when they need an ally.

They instilled strength when I wanted to give up.

"For the love of my children, I will fight any battle."
—Unknown

Ally 4

Husband

He handed me self-assurance, the ability to recognize accomplishments and have confidence in myself.

MARK SHOWED UP IN my life as a bar patron. Due to his weird work hours, he wandered into the bar just a few hours before closing. His energetic smile and jokes always left me longing for his next visit.

At the time, he was going through big challenges, himself, including the loss of his mom, his dad, and his sister, followed by a divorce, and he was raising his three children without much support.

He eagerly helped with my late-night bar duties, like stocking beer, flipping chairs, and wiping down tables. This typically was a slow time at the bar, so we had a chance to chat about divorce—I was dealing with my first, and he had just finalized his. I really appreciated his pieces of advice for navigating the nastiness of divorce.

Oftentimes, after I locked up, he made sure I made it safely to my car. He was a strong, confident, kind soul. His work ethic and commitment to his kids were other things I admired about him. I couldn't afford vacations for my girls, so I lived vicariously through him as he told me about their winter getaways to Colorado and summers spent renting a lake home. He cruised with friends in the Caribbean, went scuba diving, and owned a Harley. He lived a life I could only dream of.

Casually, he asked me out soon after my first divorce was finalized. I politely declined for a few reasons. First, he was eleven years older than I, and second, I thought he was kidding—his funny sense of humor caused me to question his seriousness.

Then, I met and married Hubby Number Two. Mark and his girlfriend, at the time, attended our wedding. I can even remember what they gave us for a wedding gift-sheets!

After we had a platonic friendship for ten years, I finally married my best friend, Mark. He saved me from the monsters that kept me in battle. When he offered his hand in marriage, it wasn't just a ring. It became the love I needed to discover confidence in myself.

Fortunately, I also gained a stepdaughter, Erin, who calls me "bonus mom." We are very good friends. Her three daughters have busy lives full of soccer, volleyball, choir, and work. The oldest just turned twenty-one! We enjoy watching their activities and playing games with them on the weekends. I also have two step sons who are middle aged.

Mark was not a Man Monster; as I described in that chapter, he was someone who appeared in my life as a partner after my saga of multiple marriages. When I struggled, he grounded me by reminding me about what I had achieved versus focusing on the undone. His morning reminders to quit regretting and start living helped me go on.

He flipped the switch on my mindset around the Money Monster by waking me up to the fact that all my hard work with home buying, remodeling, and decorating had brought us to where we are today, financially. Whenever I looked in the mirror with disgust, he would hold my naked body and remind me how beautiful I am.

The Alcohol Monster got to both of us, but it also brought us together, when he walked into my life through the door of a bar. That battleground proved messy, but together, we made it to victory. We now look at each other and say, "We saved each other." And we did!

When I asked him why he believed in me, he replied, "You were smart, pretty, and a hard worker. You ran that bar and didn't take any shit from anyone." I now trust my abilities to handle future battles, because I know I am a *Badass*!

> *You are perfect. To think anything less is as pointless as a river thinking that it's got too many curves or that it moves too slowly or that its rapids are too rapid. Says who? You're on a journey with no defined beginning, middle or end. There are no wrong twists and turns. There is just being. And your job is to be as you as you can be. This is why you're here. To shy away from who you truly are would leave the world you-less. You are the only you there is and ever will be. I repeat, you are the only you there is and ever will be. Do not deny the world its one and only chance to bask in your brilliance.*
>
> —Jen Sincero, *You Are a Badass®: How to Stop Doubting Your Greatness and Start Living an Awesome Life*

Ally 5

Tribe

They gave me a sense of belonging, that feeling of security, support, and acceptance.

OVER THE COURSE OF my life as a social butterfly, my wings grew with the energy I received from others. I loved being the party planner and couldn't wait for our next gathering. I never understood introverts. When I was younger, I had a large group of friends. The more the merrier! But after my battles, I have come to realize that that is not necessarily the case. The friends whom I thought would grow old with me are no longer in my life, because our journey is full of seasons that pass, and the same applies to friends.

We all need layers of people in our circle. The closer you get to the middle, the fewer there are. That is where you will find my tribe. Even though I have several friends in that inner circle, a book and the Universe brought me very close to two of them.

I met Barb when we lived at the Lake of the Ozarks. We hit it off quickly, as her high energy vibe matched mine. Our friendship grew over a few years. While we were visiting Barb in Arizona, before we purchased our winter home, I was introduced to her neighbor, Deloria. She had a podcast and asked us to be guests. The topic revolved around all things girly. I had dreamed of having a podcast one day, so I was all in!

Over the next couple of days, the three of us chatted about the details and quickly realized we were forming a bond. The morning of the recording, Barb brought a book, *A Tribe Called Bliss* by Lori Harder, she had just picked up from the library. She loved reading personal development books, just like I did, and had discovered that this book required the reader to find a group of two or three others to join in reading it simultaneously, sort of like a book club. The book explained that at least one reader in the group should be a newer acquaintance, since they would bring different perspectives. Deloria fit that bill 100%.

As we sat there together, we concluded the reading group would be the three of us and we would begin when I returned home, a few weeks later. As instructed in the book, we met every other week on Zoom, after reading a chapter. In those calls, we shared tears and revelations as trust grew between the three of us. One chapter was often more resonant than another, but this made us come together to support one another even more.

The bond we formed over the next year became more than any of us bargained for. Over the past three years, we have read this book several times, and every time we do, it reads differently for each of us, since we have evolved immensely.

We treasure the time we get to be together in person during the winter months in Arizona. We all kick off the year with vision boards, looking at ways to improve and make more shit happen! I know, if it weren't for those two women, the tribe book, and our consistent Zoom chats, I wouldn't be writing this book. They made me confront the monsters and held my hand as I navigated the battles.

I am forever grateful for them, as well as several other people who have lifted me up from the places of darkness. You know who you are, and I love and appreciate you just as much!

Their allegiance has given me the guidance I needed to find my true self.

> "We are the sum of all people we have ever met; you change the tribe and the tribe changes you."
> —Dirk Wittenborn

ALLY 6

BIOLOGICAL FATHER

*He provided me the opportunity to forgive,
to let go of resentment and anger.*

I HAVE NO HARD FEELINGS about the decisions my biological father, Dennis, made when he was twenty years old. As I can look back on my own life, Lord knows, I am no saint.

After I found out that I was being raised by someone other than my birth father, I knew, someday, I might meet him, but obviously, I was too young to know when. My mom wasn't in contact with him, but some of my extended family back in Washington did catch glimpses of his whereabouts on occasion.

One summer when I was a teenager, the family was looking at some old black-and-white slides on a home projector at my grandma's house. We did this often when my mom and her three brothers got together. Then, one photo popped up, and the room went silent. My aunt was running the slide show, and she immediately got the stink eye from others in room. It was my biological father's picture on the screen. She quickly went on to the next slide. This event triggered my curiosity.

As my senior spring break neared, I considered various options for that week. My mom wasn't allowing me to go with my friends to South Padre Island in Texas. This was an iconic spot for partygoers over spring break. Smart on her part, don't ya think?

Another option was to fly to my grandparents' house and possibly meet my biological father, Dennis. I started to ask the family more questions about him. At the same time, he had written a letter to my uncle, who had graduated high school with him. Their twentieth-class reunion was approaching, and Dennis hoped the letter he gave my uncle would make its way to my mom.

Well, it did! He stated he would like to meet me, probably because my eighteenth birthday was coming up-I assume. I don't recall how this all came together, but over that spring break, I went to meet my biological father for the first time. My thoughts raced before I got there.

What would he be like?

Would he look like me?

Act like me?

Did he expect me to have a relationship with him?

So much to think about!

He agreed to pick me up at my grandparents' house. They said it would be okay if he did, but I think my grandma really didn't want to see him again. I don't blame her. When he arrived, to sum it up, he looked like a mountain man: cowboy hat, jeans, boots, and a button-down shirt. No city slicker!

Physically, he did resemble me, which was reassuring. My mom is tall and has long, slender fingers, while I am short and have stubby digits. The answers I had been looking for started to appear.

Once piece of news, he told me, caught me off guard. I had a half-sister! This sparked joy for me, as, growing up, I'd always wanted a sister yet only had a little brother. Do all girls desire sisterhood? Maybe it's just me. This sister from the same mister didn't live with him, either, so she wasn't there that day. We ate lunch and then went shopping. He wanted to buy me something for my eighteenth birthday.

The following summer, I flew back to Washington and met Dennis's parents. They picked me up from my grandparents' house and drove me six hours east, through the mountains, to where Dennis lived. The driveway to his house seemed like a million miles long. When I arrived, I felt lightheaded. Clearly, this altitude was a new high for me. It felt very overwhelming to meet all these people who had been eager to meet me for many years.

Dennis lived in a beautiful log home that he had built; it was surrounded by trees and had stunning views. He also built the general store in his small town. Simple life, for sure!

After growing up in the suburbs, this world seemed quite foreign to me, but I loved it. The air smelled crisp, the people were so down to earth, and there was no traffic or busy streets. I was driven back to my grandparents' house and flew home to Kansas.

After that visit, we rarely spoke, but I reached out after my daughter's first birthday. We reunited for just a quick afternoon visit. He had moved back to the city and had a new wife. As time went on and life got busier for me, the memory of him and our visits faded. Kids, work, life, etc.

Then, one afternoon when I was in my mid-thirties, I received a phone call from him. It threw me for a loop as to why. Twenty-four years had passed so quickly without any contact. He called to inform me about a family medical condition that had been discovered when his brother got sick. We made some small talk for a bit, not really knowing what to say, and then he explained what they had found out. His brother was diagnosed with hemochromatosis which is a genetic disorder where the body absorbs too much iron. I informed my doctor, he checked my blood and nothing was out of the norm.

Now that I had his number, I thought maybe we would stay in touch. I felt the ball had been passed to my court, which was how I liked it. I wasn't ready for a commitment to a relationship, at this point. Life went on, and our conversation quickly faded to a distant memory. At some point, Dennis appeared on Facebook. He was able to keep tabs on what I had going on in my life, but we still weren't connecting.

On my fiftieth birthday, during Covid, I got a phone call from Dennis to wish me a happy birthday. I didn't answer the phone, though, figuring I would call him back another day, now that I had his new number. As I continued into my early fifties, I kept thinking about calling him. The thought of something happening to him and me not taking the initiative to call him back bothered me.

In October 2023, my uncle died, so my mom and I flew to Washington to attend the funeral. There were many familiar faces in the church, since it was the congregation, my family had grown up in. Suddenly, a man I had never seen before was standing in front of me, saying, "I could tell you were his daughter from across the room."

He turned out to be a longtime friend of Dennis's, and he had been chatting with my mom before he approached me. As we finished our conversation, I told him to have Dennis call me. Two weeks later, while I was getting my hair colored, I received a call from an unknown number. It had a Washington area code, so I answered, and yep, it was Dennis. We scheduled a time for me to call him back later that same evening.

Once we finally connected, the words flowed very naturally, and our call lasted for hours. We set up a Facetime call for the following week. I started to feel as if I had known Dennis all my life, as we connected on so many levels.

The following March, Dennis and his wife, Connie, drove down to Arizona to meet us. I had not seen my biological father in thirty-two years at that point. Our stories and laughs flowed non-stop. Mark sat there in disbelief as he observed all the many little idiosyncrasies Dennis, and I shared.

After that two-week visit, we vowed to stay in touch. Dennis and Connie also secured a place to rent in our Arizona community for the three-month 2025 winter season. That following fall, they joined Mark and I just outside Yellowstone for a week-long vacation. Later this year, Mark and I are going to Washington to see his house and the new log cabin he has been building in the mountains. I have not personally met my half-sister, as she is busy with her family, but I hope to meet her this fall. She lives only three hours away from Dennis. In the pictures I've seen of her, there is no denying we are sisters.

For most of my life, I have struggled with being so different from my mom, even though she raised me. And not just in our physical attributes, but our personality traits. My biological father, whom I now call Dad, is blonde, short, stocky, and has fat fingers. He is one of the biggest social butterflies I know. And there are other similarities, like he was a real estate agent, played softball, loves to be outside, and hates traffic and pretzels. Just like me!

Our relationship is so fun. I have a new friend in my dad, along with his wife, Connie.

Forgiving him is what I needed to do to forgive myself for the past.

FINDING HER

SECTION 3
HER WEAPONS

"My wounds have now all turned to scars."
—Author unknown

FINDING HER

Weapon 1

Books

PERSONAL DEVELOPMENT is not linear. It is a lifelong journey, and the pursuit of knowledge is a key part of growth. The following is a list of books that have left a lasting impression on me. My hope is they will provide valuable insights, strategies, and wisdom to guide you on your own path to self-discovery. These have played a significant role in defeating my monsters, so I believe they can provide you with inspiration as well as other tools to battle yours.

I put this list into sections as an easy guide for you or anyone else struggling with similar issues, so it is categorized by the monster each book assisted in slaying. Many books were helpful in multiple ways and no one book dealt directly with the Men Monsters, probably because I wasn't yet aware of that monster, when choosing my self-help books. Now that it is clearer to me, my next visits to the bookstore will be to discover more. Again, there is no end to learning more about oneself.

> "I went to a bookstore and asked the saleswoman,
> 'Where's the self-help section?'
> She said if she told me, it would defeat the purpose."
> —George Carlin

Money, Jobs and Business

Fear is not the Boss of You, Jennifer Allwood
You are a Badass at Making Money, Jen Sincero
Get Rich, Lucky Bitch, Denise Duffield-Thomas
Think and Grow Rich, Napoleon Hill
Money and The Law of Attraction, Esther & Jerry Hicks
The 12 Week Year, Brian P. Moran & Micheal Lennington
Girl Code, Cara Alwill Leyba
The Miracle Morning, Hal Elrod
The Energy Bus, Jon Gordon
The Magic of Thinking Big, David J. Schwartz
Today Matters, John C. Maxwell
#GirlBoss, Sophia Amoruso

Food & Diet

The Carnivore Diet, Dr. Shawn Baker
Grain Brain, David Perlmutter, MD
Toxic Superfoods, Sally K. Norton, MPH
Carnivore in the Kitchen, Courtney Luna
Fast, Feast, Repeat, Gin Stephens
Delay, Don't Deny, Gin Stephens
Sugar Crush, Dr. Richard Jacoby & Raquel Balderlomar
Nourishing Broth, Sally Fallon Morell & Kaayla T. Daniel

Mindset, Body Image and Self-Acceptance

You are a Badass, Jen Sincero
75 Hard, Andy Frisella
Bare, Raina O'Dell (my book coach)
The Less Effect, Samantha Joy (Owner, Landon Hail Press)
1000 Words, Jami Attenberg
A Tribe Called Bliss, Lori Harder
Girl, Wash your Face, Rachel Hollis
Girl, Stop Apologizing, Rachel Hollis
The Subtle Art of Not Giving a Fuck, Mark Manson
Fearless and Fabulous, Cara Alwill Leyba
Loving What Is, Byron Kathie & Stephen Mitchell

Gut Health & Cannabis

Wheat Belly, Dr. William Davis
Super Gut, Dr. William Davis
Buddha Belly, Brittney L. Prendergast, CHC
The Vagus Nerve Gut Brain Connection, Wendy Hayden
You Can Heal Your Life, Louise Hay
Heal Your Body, Louise Hay
Midlife Magic, Kim Sarsons
Cannabis is Medicine, Bonni Goldstein, MD
Weed Mom, Danielle Simone Brand
Cannabis for Health, Mary Clifton MD & Barbra Brownell Grogan
A Women's Guide to Cannabis, Nikki Furrer

Alcohol

This Naked Mind, Annie Grace
A Happier Hour, Rebecca Weller

Weapon 2

Podcasts

Podcasts have become one of the easiest ways to access knowledge without having to take time out to sit and read. I listen for a variety of reasons, but like my love of reading self-help, my preferences in podcasts are similar.

Typically, I like to listen to my favorites while out running errands in my car, but when we are traveling long distances, like driving to our home in Arizona, Mark and I will pick one we both enjoy.

Podcasts also provide a platform for people like myself to share our stories and insights. I've had the privilege of being a guest on several podcasts in the past, and I look forward to appearing on more, once my book is published.

"Listening to podcast, reading a book, listening to an audiobook, and watching films isn't waste of time.
It's how somebody becomes wise!"
– Deyth Banger

Money, Jobs and Business

The Jennifer Allwood Show, Jennifer Allwood
Chill & Prosper, Denise Duffield Thomas

Food & Diet

Well Beyond 40, J.J. Virgin
The Flipping 50 Show, Debra Atkinson
The Model Health Show, Shawn Stevenson
The Plant Free MD, Anthony Chaffee
The Primal Podcast, Rina Ahluwalia
The Road to Carnivore, Joanne Ozug

Mindset, Body Image and Self-Acceptance

Detached, Samantha Joy
A Women's World with Heather Dawn
The Dr. Drew Podcast, Dr. Drew Pinsky

Weapon 3

Meditation

MEDITATION HAS BEEN a weapon I have used in times of stress and anxiety. When my brain is reeling and feels like it is spinning out of control, I can sit, close my eyes, and concentrate on my breathing. This helps me focus on the task at hand.

While I was writing this book, part of my morning routine included a ten-minute meditation, followed by reading for a few minutes. This alerted my mind and body that it was time to get creative and write.

In the "Sanctuary" chapter, you can see this weapon's profound effect on how this book came together.

There are many free guided meditations available online. I prefer to use headphones to listen, while I sit in a dark room with a candle lit. When I close my eyes, I can imagine the light from the flame, and that gives me a place to focus. I hope you enjoy the journey of the mind as much as I do.

"We often experience life as a series of ups and downs, highs and lows. But if we can consistently return to center, we'll be more peaceful and less reactive, resting in the eye of the storm."
—Jay Shetty

YouTube

Positive Suggestions, www.youtube.com/@PositiveSuggestion
Boho Beautiful Yoga, www.youtube.com/@bohobeautiful
Great Meditation, www.youtube.com/@GreatMeditation

Weapon 4

Yoga

OVER THE PAST TWO years, yoga has become an important part of my morning routine. I wake up, brush my teeth, and then head to my yoga mat. My day doesn't seem to go as well, if I skip it. It is my gift to myself.

Afterward, I feel more centered, and my body appreciates these movements to start the day. Mark joins me, as well, which I love. We typically practice more of the stretchy yoga, but a few days a week, we do include yogalates, which is a combination of yoga and Pilates, for a little core challenge.

If we have a specific body part that needs more attention, we search on YouTube for a video that fits our needs. We have a few favorite instructors, and we tend to gravitate toward them, especially the ones with a soothing voice who play nice background music.

I encourage you to try yoga, if you don't currently practice it. Start with five minutes each morning and work your way up from there. Evening is another great time, too. Yoga can relax your body and help you sleep more soundly. Namaste.

"It is through the alignment of the body that I discovered the alignment of my mind, self and intelligence."

"Your body exists in the past and your mind in the future. In yoga they come together in the present."
—B. K. S. Iyengar, *Light on Yoga*

YouTube

Yoga with Joelle, www.youtube.com/@YogawithJoelle
Yoga with Kassandra, www.youtube.com/@yogawithkassandra
Yoga with Bird, www.youtube.com/@YogaWithBird
Boho Beautiful Yoga, www.youtube.com/@bohobeautiful
Yoga with Adriene, www.youtube.com/@yogawithadriene
Strengthen with Sarah, www.youtube.com/@strengthenwithsarah
Move with Nicole, www.youtube.com/@MoveWithNicole
Lidia Mera, www.youtube.com/@lidiavmera

Beachbody on Demand also has great options for Yoga.

Weapon 5

Workouts

WORKING OUT HAS BEEN a consistent part of my day for the past ten years. It's not just about changing what I look like physically, though. For me, exercise helps me mentally by relieving stress while it lets me take time for myself.

I enjoy working out at home, but I also go the local community center. Pilates and the other classes I participate in are a way for me to connect with other like-minded people and make new friends.

I use the Beachbody workout programs at home. I will list below the ones I have completed and love, even though I am no longer affiliated with this company.

There are many free online workouts on YouTube, as well. I prefer using dumbbells over big equipment, and I love lifting weights the most.

In the past, the treadmills, ellipticals and other contraptions have turned into places for me to hang my clothes. They work for many people but are not my preference.

Mark also joins me for these workouts, which helps me stay motivated and focused. I recommend finding a workout buddy—it really helps!

"The pain you feel today is the strength you feel tomorrow."
—Stephen Richards

Beachbody Programs

Les Mills Pump
21 Day Fix
21 Day Fix Extreme
80 Day Obsession
Body Beast
Liift4
10 Rounds
Morning Meltdown 100
Dig Deeper
Real Time 645
Chop Wood Carry Water

Weapon 6

Mocktails

MOCKTAILS ARE NON-ALCOHOLIC beverages designed to resemble traditional cocktails. They look like them and often taste like them, too. Mark and I enjoy having one of these concoctions a few times a week, during Happier Hour. (This is what I call it, since I am truly happier not consuming alcohol during this hour… or anytime.)

When we first quit drinking, we tried many different types of non-alcoholic liquor, beer, and wines. But now, due their sugary, carb-filled content, we simply have a flavored seltzer water, instead. We do get a bottle of (non-alcoholic) bubbly for special occasions. Cheers!

We are fortunate to have a liquor store in Missouri and Arizona called Total Wine & More. They have a wide large variety of non-alcoholic options. Amazon has a selection, too. Though Mark and I have tried many of these, below I list the ones we think are worth mentioning, in our opinion. I have still not found a non-alcoholic dry red or white wine that is worth drinking.

"Mocktails: the non-alcoholic drink for those who are hungover on life."
—Author Unknown

Beer

Hellraiser Dark Amber, Well Being Brewery
Corona NA, Constellation Brands
IPNA, Lagunitas Brewing Company
Flying Start, Boulevard Brewery
Hoppy Refresher, Lagunitas Brewing Company

Liquor

Coconut rum, Beckett's '27
Zero-proof Rum, Ritual
Amaretto, Beckett's '27
Zero-proof Tequila: Ritual
The Spirit of Tequila, Free Spirits

Sparkling Wine

Almost Zero Dry Sparking Wine
Gruvi Drysecco
Be Well Brut Rosé

ANGIE LICKLITER

Weapon 7

Cannabis

CANNABIS HAS BEEN CALLED many names over the years: pot, weed, marijuana, the devil's lettuce, ganja, bud, grass, reefer, and Mary Jane, just to name a few. When I was back in high school, we called it pot, but it was used for the psychedelic effects, not for its healing properties.

It wasn't until 1988 that a scientist discovered the endocannabinoid system. This is a complex cell-signaling system that plays a large role in regulating various things like appetite (referred to as the munchies back in my day), pain, and immune function. The active compounds found in cannabis, called cannabinoids, such as THC and CBD, interact with this system. That is why cannabis is used for medical purposes and can help manage pain, anxiety, and inflammation. Most doctors are not even aware of these properties or know very little about this plant, since nothing is taught about it in medical school.

I could go on for days about the science behind this plant. That curriculum section of my cannabis schooling was my favorite, despite the fact I hated science in high school. Cannabis still has a negative stigma, but from what

I have experienced personally, it does more positive things than negative, if used correctly.

Cannabis contains at least 113 cannabinoids (group of compounds) but below is a list of the most commonly used plus the symptoms they can help with.

> "Stress is the greatest killer worldwide, and I still believe the best medicine is and always has been marijuana."
> —Willie Nelson

> "I think people need to be educated concerning the reality that hemp isn't a drug. It is a flower and a herb. God planted it on the planet. If He planted it here and wants it to blossom, what right does the government have to think that God is mistaken?"
> —Willie Nelson

These are non-psychoactive:
- CBD-Cannabidiol: Anxiety reduction, pain reliever, seizure reduction
- CBN-Cannabinol: Neuroprotection, increases appetite, sleep benefits
- CBG-Cannabigerol: Reduces inflammation, antibacterial properties, pain reliever

This is the psychoactive one:
- THC-tetrahydrocannabinol: pain, anxiety, sleep, PTSD

SECTION 4
HER SANCTUARIES

FINDING HER

Sanctuary 1

The Cabin

A SANCTUARY REFERS TO a place of safety or protection. It can also be a personal haven where someone feels secure and at peace.

A cabin, tucked away in the mountains, became my sanctuary. Not because of its location, but because of the quiet that allowed for reflection and healing.

Are you confused about my mentioning a cabin here? Well, I don't blame you, as it was a big surprise to me, as well. Let me explain...

Earlier in the book, I described going to a meditation retreat the weekend after taking the writing class, which encouraged me to pick up the pen again. I only mentioned how the facilitator had journals and pens for us to use during the retreat. What I left out was the vision I had during the meditation. I get chills and goosebumps thinking about it.

Let me set the stage. I spent this unforgettable afternoon in a yoga studio, with my stepdaughter, a friend, and a few other women I had never met before.

It was a dark room, lit with candles, that smelled of incense. We had brought our own yoga mats, cozy blankets, and pillows, and we laid them in a half circle around a small stage where the instructor sat.

Her voice was calm, and the ambiance was very Zen-like! Nikki introduced herself and reviewed the agenda. She explained we would explore a few different forms of meditation and learn some stress-relief techniques like EFT tapping.

The first meditation would be self-led, which is what I typically practice. This form of meditation gives you guidance but then allows for quiet time, so your mind can do its thing. The second meditation would be accompanied by a sound bath and a journey through her words. I grew excited to start this mindful day. I love this kind of stuff!

We lay on the floor, with our mats underneath our bodies, covered in warm blankets, and our head supported on a pillow. We closed our eyes, and she began. Nikki softly spoke and led our minds to a place we felt safe. We were allowed to pick where that was, and mine, in the past, usually was the beach, where the sun shone warm rays upon my face.

As I settled into meditation, something in my head urged me to go another direction. It led me up a rocky, dirt path to a log cabin nestled in the woods. I loved this vision, as I take a yearly trip to Colorado with my girlfriends and stay in an Airbnb cabin in the woods, where we go hiking. So, it resonated with me deeply.

The door opened, and I walked in. To the right was a small U-shaped kitchen. As I continued toward it, I could see floor-to-ceiling windows overlooking the snow-filled mountains. Yes, it was that vivid! I continued to the left, where a ginormous stacked-stone fireplace roared with flames. I stood in front of it warming, my hands.

When I looked over, Mark stood next to me, offering me a cup of hot coffee, but only as a comforting presence in the background, not as a main character. I held onto the perfectly shaped mug and stared into the fire, while sipping my delicious coffee. Then, I looked down at what I had on. It felt and looked like a fur pelt or blanket. As I tried to comprehend what all of this meant, while remaining in a meditative state, suddenly, the fur dropped to the floor, and I was naked underneath.

Then I heard, "You are beautiful. You are beautiful," from a voice I didn't recognize. It kept repeating these words as I walked to the window to watch the snow fall. I wanted to stay and take it in for longer, but suddenly, I was diverted back to the front door.

The cabin was ready for me to leave, but I felt naked and afraid. I reluctantly opened the door and discovered a different view: a meadow of green grass and vibrant flowers.

The voice said, "Go as you are. You are beautiful. You are perfect." I walked out and then woke up from my meditative state.

Do you have chills now? I sat up, silent and reeling from what just transpired. Immediately, I grabbed my journal and began to scribble notes. I couldn't get the ink on the paper fast enough. This is what came to me:

Acceptance in a place of warmth and coziness.

Love all around me, warmth, fireplace, and coffee waiting.

I am safe but naked and covered with fur.

Snow, cold out there.

It's OK to be naked... no one cares.

You are beautiful. You are beautiful. You are beautiful.

Walk outside.

You are perfect.

I am in the place I was supposed to be.

Nikki asked if anyone wanted to share what we had visualized. Out of nowhere, I felt overwhelmed with tears and a sense of comfort. After I composed myself enough to speak, I told the participants what I had just experienced.

Everyone's eyes were wide-open in amazement, including Nikki's.

I spent the rest of the day in a daze of relaxation. When I returned home, I shared my day with Mark and cried once again.

Sanctuary 2

Herself

THAT NEXT WEEK, not knowing what lay ahead, I questioned how or if this would fit into a book, if I ever wrote one.

I began to write and expound, as I reflected on this monumental meditation...

She didn't end up at the top of the mountain, in front of this cabin, without a struggle. That is what it took for her to figure out the path. With each battle won, the right way to go grew clearer. Along the climb, she faced different obstacles, but they were manageable. She knew that challenges were a part of life's journey.

The Monsters had their own way of scaring her back into hiding. Some of their tactics filled her with unworthiness, self-doubt, disbelief, and confusion. She would do things to impress upon herself that she was okay, like getting a tattoo on her wrist. The Monsters inside were telling a different story. For her to be victorious, she had to combat them all and take the first step into the cabin, where she was accepted. Her subconscious mind had finally prevailed.

FINDING HER

She is at peace. She is warm. She is smiling. She is perfect.

Once at the cabin, she turned back to see the path. The wind had blown, covering her tracks. It was meant to be forgotten. Looking back brings tears, since leaving the old seems strange. As the tears rolled down her cheeks, they froze. She was cold. It was a nudge that it was time to go in.

She knocked on the door to confirm this was really happening, since nothing had felt like this before. The door instantly opened from the force of the knock. That became her welcome sign to enter. She took a deep breath. It smelled of wood.

The room felt so cozy, it dried her once-frozen tears and warmed her toes. No shoes needed, as the battle was over. Suddenly, as she closed her eyes and took another cleansing breath, her cold body was now covered with warmth. *What is this?* she thought. It weighed heavy on her but was soft to the touch. She opened her eyes to see the brown fur wrapping her like a hug, embracing her with love.

At first, she thought the one placing the fur resembled all of those who had helped her along the journey. She was wrong. As she stood there by the cozy fire, she realized it resembled a pelt—her warrior pelt!

She turned her head, and Mark was standing there. No words were spoken as he was there for support and love. He offered her a HOT cup of coffee, as he knew her well. You see, he had always seen the true Angie, even when she couldn't. He'd told her this repeatedly in the past, but until she could see it for herself, she couldn't receive it.

Angie pulled the fur back and extended her arm to accept this token of love.

As they both stood in front of the fire, staring at the glow, her attention turned toward the big windows. Snow is falling, and the whole picture of what this meant became clearer and clearer. You see, Angie had dreams of a cabin with a big fireplace, coffee, snuggles, and a winter wonderland around her.

In this space, the fire symbolized the burning desire she had to find herself.

The coffee represented the daily rituals in her life that she loved.

The gorgeous view through the window reflected her inner beauty.

The falling fur was the final layer she had to shed.

Over the past decade, she had created vision boards at the beginning of the New Year. The pictures resembling her goals that she had glued on the poster board had all come true, except for one: The Cabin. Although it was part of the board, it had a different meaning, one she was not conscious of. You see, a trip with family for the holidays is what she had envisioned. Little did she know, this cabin was only for her!

Ironically, her biological father, with whom she has recently connected with, builds log cabins and lives in one now.

As Angie walked toward the windows, she could see her reflection in the glass. It stared deep into her soul. It kept repeating, "You are beautiful, you are beautiful, you are beautiful." Not like an annoying broken record, but more like a voice from an angel—her grandma.

When she closed her eyes and let this moment sink in, her shoulders relaxed, and the fur fell to the ground. She was naked, just as she had been at the beginning of her journey—a baby.

The voices in her head were still repeating the new mantra. *You are beautiful, you are beautiful.*

She spun around with her arms spread, feeling free from judgment of what her body looked like. Dancing like no one was watching. A big smile and tears of joy streamed down her cheeks. She didn't want this moment to end. Then, she realized this was her new life, and it didn't end there at the cabin.

There turned out to be one more task at hand. As she walked toward the front door, she felt scared but stayed strong. She must go through the door, to find the path in her new life.

She slowly opened the door and reluctantly stepped outside, naked as a jaybird, to find the sun shining on her. There was green grass and beautiful flowers she could smell. Butterflies surrounded her, and the birds were singing a song.

You are beautiful. You are beautiful. You are beautiful.

This is Angie's new world.

SECTION 5
FINAL REFLECTIONS

FINDING HER

WHEN I TURN TO LOOK back, she's still there—smiling, waving me forward, and whispering, "You've got this. Keep going." She knows I'm better here, in the now, than I ever was back there.

And still, I pause. I stare. I feel a twinge in my heart, like I've left someone behind.

She thought she was so much fun. She *was* fun. She drank. She smoked. She lit up a room with her energy and wild heart. She had a crowd around her always. She loved the buzz of restaurants, the hum of bars, and the thrill of the party. She laughed louder after a few drinks and danced like no one was watching—because, with alcohol in her veins, fear didn't exist.

That girl, that version of me, was doing her best with what she had. She carried pain in ways even I didn't fully understand. She wore masks, layered on charm and chaos, to hide the ache in her gut and the war in her soul.

But now... this new me—she is quiet. She likes the silence and the stillness. She would rather watch the sun dip behind the mountains than hear bass thump through bar walls. She craves fresh air, the scent of pine, and the way dirt feels beneath hiking boots. Her sanctuary is under the stars, not neon lights. She drinks hot tea and sleeps deeply. No more pounding headaches, no more spinning rooms. She wakes up clear. Present. Whole.

She's not running anymore.

Her circle is smaller now—intentionally so. The ones who remain see her, truly see her. And, more important, she sees herself. Her Crohn's disease, the monster that used to call the shots, no longer has a seat at her table. She quit drinking over three years ago, and there's no going back—because she knows that one sip is a door to a place she never wants to visit again.

Still... I miss her. The old me. Maybe because she was there for so long. Maybe because letting go of her feels like a funeral for a version of myself who once made it all feel bearable. It's strange to grieve someone you used to be while also celebrating who you've become.

But that's what growth does—it births something new, while quietly saying goodbye to what was.

This season I'm in feels like a liminal space. Like late August—when the heat still lingers, but there's a whisper of fall in the air. You want to move forward, but part of you clings to the warmth. That's how this feels. A season of change. And change is never comfortable. It stretches us. It confuses us. But it also refines us.

The truth is, if I were still the old me, I wouldn't be writing this book. I wouldn't have had the clarity or courage. I wouldn't have the freedom in my mornings or the fire in my soul to put these words to paper. Those old habits would've robbed me of this voice.

So, why do I keep glancing back?

Maybe because change doesn't happen all at once. Maybe because I'm still growing into this version of me. Maybe because I'm finally allowing myself to feel it all—the loss and the gain.

I'm not broken. I'm evolving.

I don't want to go back. But I do want to understand why I keep looking. And perhaps it's not to return... but to remember. To honor her. To thank her for getting me here.

Because she did. She carried the weight until I was strong enough to set it down.

And now... I see the path ahead. It's new. It's unfamiliar. But it's mine. I won't need to keep looking behind me, because what's coming is far too bright to miss.

There are big things headed my way. I feel it deep in my gut—the same gut that once ached from disease now pulses with intuition.

And then she came—the one without a name.

The one who lived buried, waiting.

The one who always knew there was more.

She was never lost... only hidden.

Angie is the weapon.

All she needed was to Find Her.

FINDING HER

"I was looking for someone to inspire me, motivate me, support me, keep me focused... Someone who would love me, cherish me, make me happy, and I realized, all along, I was looking for myself."
—Unknown

If you're interested in learning more
about Angie's coaching,
Or looking for a speaker for your next
event or podcast, please visit:

www.AngieLickliter.com

Email: Angie@angielickliter.com
Follow @Angie_Lickliter on Instagram
Follow @Angie Lickliter on Facebook

Acknowledgments

WELL, HERE WE ARE... A finished book. *Who knew?* (Besides the Universe, who's been nudging me for years to "just write the thing.")

First, a huge thank-you to Samantha Joy at Landon Hail Press, my fabulous publisher. You saw something in this story (and in me) and said, "Let's do this!" Your belief and guidance helped bring this dream to life.

To my book coach, Raina O'Dell—you lit a fire under my writing butt and reminded me that my story matters. Thank you for being part cheerleader, part therapist, and part "kick you into gear" friend.

I would also like to thank Kim Sarsons, who assisted me in the "Dare the Share" project that sadly was cancelled. She helped me with the beginning stages of writing about my Gut Monster.

To Kathryn, my editor—you took my messy brain dump and helped turn it into an actual book. Your edits were like a makeover for my words—polished, but still totally me.

To my beta readers, Jamie, Dana, Tracy, and Barbra— you brave souls read the early versions and didn't run. Your honesty, kindness, and comments helped shape this into something better than I imagined.

To my mom—thanks for having me... and keeping me. That part was kind of essential.

To my daughters, Megan and Lauren—you've grown into such amazing, strong women, and I am fiercely proud of you both. Thank you for being the best chapters of my life story.

And to my husband, Mark—my ride-or-die, my sounding board, and the man who kept believing in me even when I wanted to throw my laptop out the window. You've been my biggest fan, and I love you eternally for it!

To everyone who had a hand in this—thank you from the bottom of my heart.

About the Author

ANGIE LICKLITER IS A passionate wellness advocate and entrepreneur who has dedicated much of her life to serving others. The University of Hard Knocks gave her experience in navigating life's many challenges and taught her valuable lessons. She is former coffee shop owner and a person of many talents.

At the age of twenty-seven, she was diagnosed with Crohn's disease, which drove her to explore alternative methods of healing. This sparked a desire to work in the field of wellness. She has led dozens of online support groups, educating women on subjects such as clean eating, portion control, and workout programs to achieve their desired health and fitness goals. Her certifications from the Holistic Wellness Coaching Academy and the Cannabis Coaching Institute inspired her to create Gut Girl Coaching, where she guided clients to achieve optimal well-being, utilizing holistic approaches.

Now, as the author of *Finding Her*, Angie leverages her twenty-five-plus years of managing Crohn's disease and her lifelong battles related to food, alcohol, and men, to encourage her readers to discover their warrior within and take control of their life.

She and her husband enjoy traveling, hiking, golf, pickleball, and spending time with family. Their home base is Raymore, Missouri, but they venture to Casa Grande, Arizona during the cold months to keep the winter blues away. They share five adult children, six grandchildren, and will be celebrating their twenty-year wedding anniversary next year.

www.ingramcontent.com/pod-product-compliance
Lightning Source LLC
LaVergne TN
LVHW011415080426
835512LV00005B/78